Learn Intermediate Spanish In 30 Days: The Beginners Language Learning Accelerator- Short Stories, Common Phrases, Grammar, Conversations, Essential Travel Terms& Words In Context

TABLE OF CONTENTS

Introduction 8

I. Bases del español (Basics of Spanish) 12

    1. Pronombres personales / Personal Pronouns...... 12

    2. Artículos definidos e indefinidos / Definite and Indefinite Articles 13

    3. Géneros / Genders 14

    4. Estructuras singulares y plurales (Singular and plural estructures) 15

    5. Los adjetivos / The adjectives 15

    7. Partículas interrogativas.. 17

II. Los verbos en Español / The verbs in Spanish 19

    1. Verbos de primer grupo (First group verbs)......... 19

    2. Verbos de segundo grupo (Second group verbs) . 20

    3. Verbos de tercer grupo (Third group verbs) 21

    4. Oraciones afirmativas, negativas e interrogativas – *Affirmative, Negative and Interrogative Sentences* . 22

III. Los verbos irregulares / The irregular verbs .. 25

    1. Verbos ir / venir (Verbs "to go / to come") 25

    2. Verbos comunes irregulares.................................. 26

IV. La perífrasis verbal / Verbal Periphrasis 28

V. Verbos copulativos "ser y estar" / Copulative verbs "ser and estar" 30

    1. Verbo "ser" – Verb "ser" 30

    Verbo "estar" – Verb "estar" 31

    Vocabulario 32

    Vocabulario 33

VI. Verbos reflexivos / Reflexive verbs 35

    Verbos reflexivos de rutina diaria (Daily routine reflexive verbs) 35

    Verbos no reflexivos de rutina diaria (Non-reflexive daily routine verbs) 36

    Verbo quedar vs quedarse 37

    Verbo "parecer" vs "parecerse" 38

    Verbo encontrar vs encontrarse 39

    Verbo "ir" vs "irse" 40

VII. Adjetivos posesivos / Possessive Adjectives 42

    Vocabulario 43

    Vocabulario 45

    Algunas nacionalidades (Some nationalities) 47

VIII. Preposiciones – Prepositions 50

    Vocabulario 51

    Vocabulario 56

IX. Los números y la fecha / The numbers and the date 59

1. Los números (Numbers) 59
2. Los días de la semana (The days of the week) 60
3. Meses del año 61

X. Adjetivos demostrativos / Demonstrative adjectives 64

XI. Verbo "Gustar" / Verb "to like" 68

Vocabulario 69

Vocabulario 71

XII. Comparaciones / Comparisons 73

Oraciones comparativas / Comparative sentences .. 73

Oraciones superlativas / Superlative sentences 74

Comparaciones de igualdad / *Comparisons of equality* 75

XIII. Adverbios / Adverbs 78

Adverbios de tiempo / Adverbs of time 78

Adverbios de frecuencia 79

Adverbios de lugar / *Adverbs of place* 80

Adverbios de modo / *Adverbs of manner* 80

Adverbios de aproximación 81

XIV. Tiempo presente continuo / Present continuous tense 85

Vocabulario 87

XV. Pronombres personales tónicos / Tonic personal pronouns 93

XVI. Tiempo Pasado Simple / Simple Past Tense. 104

Conjugación del verbo "-ar" / *Conjugation of the verb "-ar"* 104

Conjugación del verbo "-er" / *Conjugation of the verb "-er"* 105

Conjugación del verbo "-ir" / *Conjugation of the verb "-ir"* 106

Preguntas en Pasado Simple / *Simple Past Questions.* 108

Afirmación en Pasado Simple / *Simple past affirmation* 108

Negación en Pasado Simple / *Simple Past Negation.* 108

Verbos irregulares en tiempo pasado simple / *Irregular verbs in simple past tense* 109

XVII. Preposiciones de lugar / Prepositions of place 116

XVIII. Pronombres Posesivos / Possessive Pronouns 130

Possessive pronouns 130

XIX. The possessive using "apostrophe « s »" in Spanish... 132

XX. Los pronombres objeto directo 137

XXI. Pronombres objeto indirecto / Indirect Object Pronoun 144

XXII. Pronombre "Lo / La" vs Pronombre "Le" / Pronoun "Lo / La" vs Pronoun "Le" 149

XXIII. Religiones y doctrinas / Religions and doctrines. 153

XIV. Conectores / *Connectors.* 158

Conectores Aditivos / *Additive connectors.* 158

Conectores Adversarios / *Adversative connectors*. 160

Conectores Consecutivos / *Consecutive connectors* 161

Conectores explicativos / *Explanatory Connectors* 163

Conectores concesivos / Concessive connectors... 164

Conectores recapitulativos / Recapitulatives Connectors 164

Conectores de Ordenación / *Sort connectors* 165

XXV. Conjunciones / Conjunctions................... 167

XXVI. Verbos esenciales / Essential verbs 172

Para viajar / *For travelling* 172

Para trabajar / For working 174

Para cocinar / For cooking....................................... 175

Para conversar / *For talking* 176

Para festejar / *For partying* 177

CONCLUSION **179**

Introduction

Hola and welcome to Learn Spanish in Your Car for Beginners. First, we would like to sincerely thank you and congratulate you for having made this amazing decision of investing on this incredible book that will help you learn the foundations of Spanish while you keep going through your daily routine, driving, walking or cooking!

As we know now, Spanish has become one of the most popular languages worldwide. This is directly translated as many people willing to connect to other cultures, companies wanting to explore new markets. Artists, businesspersons, tourists, culture and language lovers feel attracted by this beautiful, creative and poetic language that is now the third most spoken language. So, *felicitaciones* again for giving the first step towards what will become a tool to connect with new opportunities!

This book will become your best partner throughout your learning process. As we go, chapter by chapter, you will have the opportunity to understand the game rules of Spanish language, which will consolidate a steady base that will allow you to grow and build an entire structure full of grammar concepts, vocabulary, tips and many hours of listening practice.

Our system

This book was created to help you learn this amazing language in the simplest way and that's why we've decided to divide every topic into different chapters that will give you the idea of what you will start learning during your daily lesson.

Throughout these chapters, you will have the opportunity to start your learning process from the very basics of Spanish, which will not only make you repeat word after word and force your brain to try to understand why, but also it will include quick notes and a highly organized structure that will clear your doubts as you listen the vocabulary.

This book will be divided into 30 chapters. Every chapter will be titled with a specific topic, like "Pronouns", for example.

At some points during the chapters, you will have the opportunity to listen to short stories or dialogues that will help you go deep into the real use of Spanish in daily-life conversations.

Some of the chapters will also include specific vocabulary that will give you extra ideas about how Spanish works and how to combine the main topics with these new words you will learn.

For each and every word, it will first be presented in it's Spanish form and then the English form. Some of the subcategories will introduce only translations and some others will contain a sentence using that particular Spanish word into context.

For dialogues and stories, you will first listen to a longer paragraph in Spanish, and then you will have to opportunity to listen to its translation in English. This as part of your system to help you accelerate your learning process and take fully advantage of these amazing 10 hours of complete audio practice that will give you a great level in Spanish in 30 days.

Finally, some of the topics will include an introductory paragraph as well as quick notes and interesting facts that will not only allow you to learn new words by listening and repeating, but also to have a full understanding of this beautiful language.

Before we begin...

We want you to know that learning a new language can be challenging and confusing at times. At Excel Language Lessons, we are focused on providing the easiest, clearest and most concise guides for beginners to learn new languages. With that being said, it is up to you to apply yourself in order to achieve your bilingual goals and become an expert through the process of reading our proven guides.

We would like to thank and congratulate you on your decision to purchase this book; it takes a lot of courage and due diligence to take on a new language!

So let's get ready and prepare our minds to start this amazing journey throughout the romantic world of español!

¡Comencemos! Let's begin!

I. Bases del español (Basics of Spanish)

1. Pronombres personales / Personal Pronouns

Yo – I
Yo soy latino
I am latino

Tú – You (informal, singular)
Tú hablas español
You speak Spanish

Él – He
Él vive en México
He lives in México

Ella – She
Ella bebe café
She drinks coffee

Nosotros, Nosotras - We (masculine or neutral and feminine form respectively)
Nosotros tenemos una casa
We have a house

Usted – You (formal, singular)
Usted es profesor
You are a professor

Ustedes – You (plural)
Ustedes bailan salsa
You guys dance salsa

Ellos – They (masculine form)
Ellos trabajan mucho
They work a lot

Ellas – They (feminine form)
Ellas son actrices
They are actresses

2. Artículos definidos e indefinidos / Definite and Indefinite Articles

El – The (singular, masculine)
El perro
The dog

La – The (singular, feminine)
La casa
The house

Los – The (plural, masculine)
Los niños
The boys

Las – The (plural, feminine)
Las niñas
The girls

Un – A / An (singular, masculine)
Un perro
A dog

Una – A / An (singular, plural)
Una casa
A house

Unos – Some (masculine)
Unos perros
Some dogs

Unas – Some (feminine)
Unas niñas
Some girls

3. Géneros / Genders

Género masculino / Masculine gender
In Spanish, letter "o" at the end of a word, creates the masculine form of a noun or adjective.
Perro / Male dog
Niño / Boy
Apartamento / Appartment
Carro / Car
Género femenino / Feminine gender

In Spanish, letter "a" at the end of a word, creates the feminine form of a noun of adjective.
Perra / Female dog
Niña / Girl
Casa / House
Bicicleta / Bicycle
Following this rule, we can combine nouns with articles, matching gender and quantity.
El perro en el apartamento - The male dog in the appartment
Un niño en la casa - *A boy in the house*
La bicicleta de la niña - *The bicycle of the girl*

4. Estructuras singulares y plurales (Singular and plural estructures)

In Spanish, as in English, letter "s" defines the plural form of all nouns and adjectives (with some exceptions).
El niño; Los niños - *The boy ; the boys*
La casa: las casas - *The house; the houses*
Un carro; unos carros - *A car; some cars*
Una manzana; unas manzanas - *An Apple; some apples*

5. Los adjetivos / The adjectives

In Spanish, adjectives have to match two specific factors: gender and quantity.
Adjetivos masculinos / Masculine adjectives
El niño alto - *The tall boy*
Los niños altos - *The tall boys*

Un apartamento bonito - *A pretty appartment*
Unos apartamentos bonitos - *Some pretty appartments*
Adjetivos femininos / Feminine adjectives
La niña alta - *The tall girl*
Las niñas altas - *The tall girls*
Una casa bonita - *A pretty house*
Unas casas bonitas - *Some pretty houses*

Vocabulario (Adjetivos) – Vocabulary (adjectives)

a. Altura y peso (height and weight)

Alto / Alta – *Tall*
Pequeño / Pequeña – *Small or Short*
Flaco / Flaca – *Skinny*
Gordo / Gorda – *Fat*
Grande – Big (both masculine and feminine)

b. Colores (Colors)

Rojo / roja – *Red*
Amarillo / amarilla – *Yellow*
Azul – blue (both masculine and feminine)
Verde – green (both masculine and feminine)
Naranja – orange (both masculine and feminine)
Morado / morada – *purple*
Blanco / Blanca – *White*
Negro / Negra – *Black*

c. Apariencia (appearance)

Bonito / bonita – *Pretty*
Hermoso / hermosa – *Beautiful*
Feo / Fea – *Ugly*

7. Partículas interrogativas

¿Qué? – What?
¿Qué hora es?
What time is it?

¿Quién? – Who?
¿Quién quiere pizza?
Who wants pizza?

¿Cómo? – How?
¿Cómo estás?
How are you?

¿Cuándo? – When?
¿Cuándo vienes a la fiesta?
When are you coming to the party?

¿Por qué? – Why?
¿Por qué aprendes español?
Why do you learn Spanish?

¿Dónde? – Where?
¿Dónde vives?

Where do you live?

Fin del capítulo / *End of chapter*

II. Los verbos en Español / The verbs in Spanish

1. Verbos de primer grupo (First group verbs)

In Spanish, verbs change their structures when conjugated. All first group verbs end with syllable "ar" and all of them —with few exceptions- are considered "regular verbs" which means, they follow the same conjugation rule.

Conjugación de verbos de primer grupo / Conjugation of first group verbs
Verbo "hablar" – "To speak"
Yo hablo - I speak
Tú hablas - You speak
Él habla - He speaks
Ella habla - She speaks
Nosotros hablamos, nosotras hablamos - We speak
Usted habla - You speak
Ustedes hablan - You speak (plural)
Ellos hablan, ellas hablan - They speak

Practica de conversación – Diálogos (Conversation practice – Dialogues)
1) ¿Tú hablas español? – *Do you speak Spanish?*

Sí, yo hablo español. – *Yes, I speak Spanish.*

2) ¿Ella baila salsa? – *Does she dance salsa?*
No, ella no baila salsa. – No, she doesn't dance salsa.

3) ¿Ustedes pintan la casa hoy? – *Do you guys paint the house today?*
Sí, nosotros pintamos la casa hoy – *Yes, we paint the house today.*

4) ¿Juan trabaja en una oficina? – *Does Juan work in an office?*
No, Juan trabaja en un hotel – *No, Juan Works in a hotel.*

Fin del diálogo– *End of the diálogo*

---

2. Verbos de segundo grupo (Second group verbs)

In Spanish, second group verbs include irregular verbs, but some others follow the same rule always.

Verbo "comer" – "To eat"

Yo como - I eat
Tú comes - You eat
Él come - He eats
Ella come - She eats
Nosotros comemos, nosotras comemos - We eat
Usted come - You eat
Ustedes comen - You eat (plural)
Ellos comen, Ellas comen - They eat

Practica de conversación – Diálogos (Conversation practice – Dialogues)

1) ¿Tú comes burritos? – *Do you eat burritos?*
Sí, me encantan los burritos. – *Yes, I love burritos.*

2) ¿Comen con nosotros esta noche? – *Do you guys eat with us tonight?*
No, no podemos – No, we can't.

3) Los niños comen muchos dulces – *Kids eat a lot of candies*
Sí, lo sé – *Yes, I know.*

Fin del diálogo– *End of the diálogo*

---

3. Verbos de tercer grupo (Third group verbs)

In Spanish, third group verbs are considered irregular verbs, as they don't follow the same conjugation rule. However, you can find multiple third groups verbs that will have the same structure.

Verbo "vivir" – To live
Yo vivo - I live
Tú vives - You live
Él vive - He lives
Ella vive - She lives
Nosotros vivimos, Nosotras vivimos - We live
Usted vive - You live

Ustedes viven - You live (plural)
Ellos viven, Ellas viven - They live

Practica de conversación – Diálogos (Conversation practice – Dialogues)

1) ¿Dónde vives tú? – *Where do you live?*
Yo vivo en Cuba. – *I live in Cuba.*

2) ¿Maria vive con su mamá? – *Does Maria live with her mom?*
Sí, ella vive con su mamá – *Yes, she lives with her mom*

3) Sr. Rodriguez, ¿usted vive solo? – *Mr. Rodriguez, do you live alone?*
Sí, yo vivo solo. – *Yes, I live alone.*

Fin del diálogo– *End of the diálogo*

---

4. Oraciones afirmativas, negativas e interrogativas – *Affirmative, Negative and Interrogative Sentences*

Introduction: In English, according to the type of sentence and verbs, you need to add auxiliar words to answer, deny and create an interrogative structure. For example, "you eat an apple" has to have an additional verb when changing into a interrogative sentence, i.e. "do you eat an apple?"

However, these additions are not necessary in Spanish, not even the common switching when using verb "to be", for example: "you are a doctor" – "are you a doctor?"
Vamos a los ejemplos / Let's go to the examples.

Oraciones afirmativas versus oraciones negativas – Negative versus affirmative sentences

Yo vivo en Honduras – *I like in Honduras*
Yo no vivo en Honduras – *I don't live in Honduras*

Maria quiere café – *Maria wants coffee*
María no quiere café – *Maries doesn't want coffee*

Nosotros bailamos salsa – *We dance salsa*
Nosotros no bailamos salsa – *We don't dance salsa*

Tú estás cansado / *You are tired*
Tú no estás cansado / *You are not tired*

Oraciones interrogativas – Interrogative sentences

¿Quieres pizza? – *Do you want pizza?*
¿Tienes hijos? – *Do you have kids?*
¿Te gusta el español? – *Do you like Spanish?*
¿Estás en México? – *Are you in Mexico?*

Respuestas – *Answers*

Sí, sí me gusta la pizza – *Yes I do like pizza*
No, no me gusta la pizza – *No, I don't like pizza*

Sí, tengo 3 hijos – *Yes, I have 3 kids*
No, no tengo hijos – No, I don't have kids

Sí, estoy en México – *Yes, I'm in Mexico*
No, no estoy en México – *No, I'm not in Mexico.*

Quick note: As you can see, answers are simple and do not require any additional word rather than *"Sí"* or *"No"*. Actually, it is completely correct to answer only by saying *"Sí / no"* without using any other verb or something similar to "I do", "I have", "I don't", "I am"…

About negative sentences, you can see that, in Spanish, you only need to add the word "no" always *before* the verb, regardless the kind of verb you are using.

Fin del capítulo / *End of chapter*

III. Los verbos irregulares / The irregular verbs

1. Verbos ir / venir (Verbs "to go / to come")
Conjugación / Conjugation
Ir (to go)
Yo voy - I go
Tú vas - You go
Él va - He goes
Ella va - She goes
Nosotros vamos, Nosotras vamos – We go
Usted va - You go
Ustedes van – You (plural) go
Ellos van, Ellas van – They go

Verbo "venir" – Verb "to come"
Conjugación – Conjugation
Yo vengo – I come
Tú vienes – You come
Él viene – He comes
Ella viene – She comes
Nosotros venimos, Nosotras venimos – We coe
Usted viene – You come
Ustedes vienen – You (plural) come
Ellos vienen, Ellas vienen – They come

Pequeña historia – Short story
Juan va; Juan viene – Juan goes; Juan comes

Todos los días, Juan va a la universidad en bus – *Every day, Juan goes to the university by bus.*
Los fines de semana, Juan va a casa de su mamá – *On weekends, Juan goes to his mom's house.*
Usualmente, Juan va a casa de su mamá en taxi – *Usually, Juan goes to his mom's house by taxi.*
Juan, ¿cuándo vienes a la casa hoy? – *Juan, When do you come home today?*
Mamá, voy a las 8:00, como siempre – *Mom, I go at 8:00, as always.*

Fin de la historia – *End of the story*

---

2. Verbos comunes irregulares

Verbos "tener, querer, hacer, poder" – *Verbs "to have, to want, to do, can / may"*

Yo puedo hablar español - *I can speak Spanish*

María quiere un trabajo nuevo – *Maria wants a new job*

¿Qué haces esta noche? – *What do you do tonight?*

¿Cuántos años tienes? – *How old are you?*

Tengo 22 años – *I'm 22 years old*

Quick note: in Spanish, they literally say: "How many years do you have?"

¿Cuántos hijos tienen ellos? – *How many kids do they have?*
Hoy queremos ir a la playa – *Today we want to go to the beach*

¿Pueden venir a la fiesta esta noche? – *Can you guys come to the party tonight?*

Normalmente yo hago todo el trabajo – *Normally I do all the work*

Quiero aprender español – *I want to learn Spanish*

IV. La perífrasis verbal / Verbal Periphrasis

Introduction: as in English, a sentence can have more than two consecutive verbal structures either to create complex tenses such as "would have done" or simpler sequences like "have to do" or "can do". These combinations are called verbal periphrasis, but in Spanish, they don't work in the same way as in English.

In Spanish there are specific rules which you will learn in this book. But, for now, you can focus on the most basic of them: When you have two verbs together, in Spanish you will only conjugate the first one and leave the second action unconjugated.

<u>*Perífrasis con "Tener que" / Periphrasis with "Have to"*</u>

Tengo que comprar comida / *I have to buy food*
Tenemos que visitar a José / *We have to visit José*
Maria tiene que ir a la playa / *Maria has to go to the beach*

<u>*Perífrasis con "Querer" / Periphrasis with "Want to"*</u>

Quiero ir a Mexico este año / *I want to go to Mexico this year*

¿Quieres cenar conmigo? / *Do you want to have pizza for dinner?*
Queremos aprender español / *We want to learn Spanish*

Perífrasis con "Poder" / Periphrasis with "Can"

¿Puedes hablar español? / *Can you speak Spanish?*
¿Puedo ir contigo a la fiesta? / *Can I go with you to the party?*
Las aves pueden volar / *Birds can fly*

Perífrasis con "ir a" / Periphrasis with "Go to"

Vas a practicar en la biblioteca / *You go to practice in the library*
María va a hacer ejercicio / *Maria goes to do exercise*
Quick note 1: This specific periphrasis works as a future tense and can be translated as "going to" in English.
Quick note 2: The English structure "Let's" as in "Let's eat" has a similar version in Spanish and it's created by conjugated "ir" with pronoun "nosotros" or "nosotras". For example:

Vamos a comer / *Let's eat*
Vamos a practicar / *Let's practice*

Fin del capítulo / *End of chapter*

V. Verbos copulativos "ser y estar" / Copulative verbs "ser and estar"

Introduction: in Spanish, the actions of being someone or something and being somewhere are explained using a different verb. Situations such as identification, description and definition will be expressed using "ser". On the other hand, from a general point of view, verb "estar" will describe location, feelings and emotions.

Both verbs "ser" and "estar" have the same translation in English: "to be" but they will be used in total different contexts and both are considered irregular verbs.

1. Verbo "ser" – Verb "ser"
Conjugación
Yo soy estudiante – *I am a student*
Tú eres bueno – You are good
Él es alto – He is tall
Ella es latina – *She is latina*
Nosotros somos argentinos – *We are Argentinians*
Usted es el señor Gonzales – You are mister Gonzales
Ustedes son amigos – You guys are Friends
Ellas son cristianas – *They are Christians*

Verbo "estar" – Verb "estar"

Conjugación

Yo estoy en Colombia – *I'm in Colombia*
Tú estás feliz – *You are happy*
Él está ocupado – *He is busy*
Ella está en la avenida Diego Fernandez – *She is in the Diego Fernandez Avenue*
Nosotros estamos cerca – *We are close*
Usted está cansado – *You are tired*
Ustedes están en México – *You guys are in Mexico*
Ellos están aquí en casa – *They are here at home.*

Pequeña historia – Short story

¿Dónde está Juan? – *Where's Juan?*

¿Dónde está tu hermano? – *Where's your brother?*
Él está en casa de Pedro – *He's at Pedro's house*
¿Quién es Pedro? – *Who's Pedro?*
Pedro es un amigo de la escuela – *Pedro is a friend from school*
Tengo que llamar a su casa, es muy tarde. Son las 10 pm. – *I have to call to his house, it's very late. It's 10 pm.*
On the phone: Hola Pedro ¿Cómo estás? – *Hi Pedro how are you?*
Estoy bien, gracias. – *I'm fine, thank you.*
¿Juan está en tu casa? – *Is Juan in your house?*
Sí, él está aquí. – *Yes, He is here*

Fin del diálogo – *End of the dialogue*

Vocabulario

Profesiones I (Professions I)

Quick note: In Spanish, most of the professions also have gender, which mean, a word like "lawyer" will have a masculine and a feminine form.

Abogado, Abogada / *Lawyer*
Maestro, Maestra / *Teacher*
Doctor, Doctora / *Doctor*
Ingeniero, Ingeniera / *Engineer*
Vendedor, Vendedora / *Seller*
Contador, Contadora / *Accountant*
Cocinero, Cocinera / *Cook*
Panadero, Panadera / *Baker*

Práctica conversación – Diálogos (Conversation practice – Dialogues)
1) ¿Cuál es tu profesión? - *What's your profession?*
Soy profesor de matemáticas - *I'm a math teacher*

2) Yo soy abogada, me gusta ayudar a otros – *I'm a lawyer, i like to help others*
¿Y te gusta tu profesión? – *And do you like your profession?*
Si, me encanta – *Yes, I love it*

3) Hoy voy a casa de un amigo, él es cocinero – *Today I go to to a friend's house, he is a cook.*
¿Puedo ir contigo? - *Can I go with you?*
Claro – *Of course*
Fin del diálogo– *End of the dialogue*

Vocabulario

<u>Emociones y sentimientos I (Emotions and feelings I)</u>

Feliz / *Happy*
Hoy estoy feliz / *I'm happy today*

Triste / *Sad*
María está triste y no sé por qué / *Maria is sad and I don't know why*

Molesto, Molesta / *Angry*
Los niños están molestos / *The kids are angry*

Cansado, Cansada / *Tired (masculine and femenine form)*
Juan está cansado. Tiene mucho trabajo / *Juan is tired. He has a lot of work*

Emocionado, Emocionada / *Excited (masculine and feminine form)*
¡Estoy muy emocionada por la fiesta! / *I'm very excited for the party!*

Quick note: there are feelings in Spanish that won't use the same verb "to be" as in English in situations like "I'm afraid" or "I'm hungry", on the contrary, in Spanish, feelings are something you literally "have", so instead of saying "being afraid", you would say "having fear" or "having hunger"

Tener frío / Being *cold*
Tengo frío / *I'm cold*

Tener calor / Being hot
Tengo calor / *I'm hot*

Tener miedo / *Being afraid or scared*
¿Tienes miedo? / *Are you afraid?*

Tener hambre / *Being hungry*
Necesito comer, tengo mucha hambre / *I need to eat, I'm very hungry*

Tener / *Being thirsty*
¿Tienes sed? ¿Quieres agua? / *Are you thirsty? Do you want some water?*

Tener sueño / *Being sleepy*
Los tienen tienen mucho sueño / *Kids are very sleepy*

Fin del capítulo / *End of chapter*

VI. Verbos reflexivos / Reflexive verbs

Introduction: In Spanish, a reflexive verb is a common form used to explain, for example, daily activities such as waking up, going to bed, brushing your teeth, and even literal reflexive actions such as looking ourselves in the mirror.

A reflexive verb is formed by the main action like "mirar" (to watch) and a reflexive pronoun or *pronombre reflexivo,* which will be placed at the end of the verb in its infinitive form, following this idea, mirar (to watch) becomes mirarse (to watch oneself).

As a last note, every personal pronoun will need a reflexive pronoun when conjugating a reflexive verb. Following the previous structures, the reflexive pronouns are: Yo me, Tú te, él se, ella se, nosotros nos, usted se, ustedes se, ellos se.

Verbos reflexivos de rutina diaria (Daily routine reflexive verbs)
Levantarse (to get up)
Yo me levanto a las 8:00 am – *I wake up at 8:00 am*

Bañarse (to take a shower)
Tú te bañas todos los días – *You take a shower every day*

Cepillarse (to brush)
Ella se cepilla los dientes después de bañarse – *She brushes the teeth after taking a shower*

Vestirse (to get dressed)

Nosotros nos vestimos antes de ir al trabajo – *We get dressed before going to work*
Dormirse (to sleep)
Ellos se duermen a las 10:00 pm – *They sleep at 10:00 pm*

Verbos no reflexivos de rutina diaria (Non-reflexive daily routine verbs)

Desayunar – To have breakfast
Almorzar – To have lunch
Cenar – To have dinner

Pequeña historia – Short story
La rutina diaria de María – Maria's daily routine
Me levanto a las 7:00 AM todas las mañanas. – *I get up at 7:00 am every morning.*
Tomo una taza de café y desayuno. – *I take a cup of coffee and I have breakfast*
Luego me baño, me cepillo mis dientes y me visto. – *Then I take a shower, I brush my teeth and I get dressed*
A las 8:00 am voy al trabajo – *At 8:00 I go to work*

Normalmente, almuerzo a las 12:00 pm. – *Normally, I have lunch at 12:00pm*
A las 5:00 pm regreso a casa – *At 5:00 pm I come back home*
A las 8:00 pm ceno. Usualmente ceno sandwhich y jugo – *At 8:00 pm I have dinner. Usually I have sandwich and juice for dinner*
Finalmente, a las 10:00 me duermo – *Finally, at 10:00 I sleep.*
Fin de la historia – *End of the story*

Verbo quedar vs quedarse

Introduction: some few verbs in Spanish will have a complete different translation depending on if they are reflexive or not. One of these examples is verb *"quedar"* and *"quedarse"*. *Vamos a comenzar. Let's begin.*

1) "Quedar": works as a synonym of "estar"

¿Dónde queda la estación de tren? / *Where's the train station?*

¿Sabes dónde queda el restaurante mexicano? / *Do you know where the mexican restaurant is?*

Mi casa queda cerca de la playa / *My house is close to the beach*

El supermercado queda lejos del hospital / *The supermarket is far from the hospital*

2) "Quedarse" / To stay

Hoy me quedo en casa de Juan / *Today I stay at Juan's house*

Los chicos se quedan en la fiesta hasta las 7 / *They guys stay in the party until 7*

En mi viaje a México me quedo en un hotel cinco estrellas / *On my trip to México I'll stay in a five-star hotel*

¿Vas a Barcelona? ¿Y dónde te quedas? – *Are you going to Barcelone? And where are you going to stay?*

Verbo "parecer" vs "parecerse"

1) Parecer / *to seem: to think*

Parece que va a llover / *It seems like it's going to rain*
Parece fácil / *It seems easy*
Me parece que el español es interesante / *It seems to me that Spanish is interesting*
¿Qué te parece si salimos mañana? / *What do you think about going out tomorrow?*
Me parece que la película es muy buena / *I think the movie is very good*

2) Parecerse / *To look like*

Yo me parezco a mi papá / *I look like my dad*
Colombia se parece a Venezuela / *Colombia looks like Venezuela*
Mi hermana no se parece a mí / *My sister doesn't look like me*
El español no se parece al inglés / *Spanish is not similar to English.*

Verbo encontrar vs encontrarse

1) Encontrar / To find

Yo necesito encontrar un trabajo / *I need to find a job*
El capitán encuentra un tesoro / *The captain finds a treasure*
El niño quiere encontrar un amigo para jugar / *The boy wants to find a friend to play with*
No encuentro las llaves / *I can't find the keys.*

2) Encontrarse / *To meet*

Mañana nos encontramos aquí a las 10 / *Tomorrow we'll meet here at 10*
Hoy me encuentro en el café con Daniel / *Today I'll meet with Daniel at the café*
¿Dónde nos encontramos? / *Where do we meet?*
Maria se encontró con su ex novio / *Maria met with her ex boyfriend*

Verbo "ir" vs "irse"

Quick note: even though in Spanish the action of "going" can be reflexive or not and still keep the same meaning, there are situations in which you can only use its reflexive form.

Ir vs Irse

Yo voy al trabajo / *I go to work*
Yo me voy del trabajo / *I go out from work*

Ella va a la casa / *She goes to the house*
Ella se va de la casa / *She goes out from home*

Mañana vamos a Italia / *Tomorrow we go to Italy*
Nos vamos de Italia mañana / *We are leaving Italy tomorrow*

Interesting fact: In Spanish, there are verbs that won't change their meaning even if you say it in a reflexive or "non-reflexive" form. Vamos a ver los ejemplos / *Let's see the examples*

Yo como una pizza / *I eat a pizza*
Yo me como una pizza / *I eat a pizza*

Juan lee un libro / *Juan reads a book*
Juan se lee un libro / *Juan reads a book*

Nosotros desayunamos a las 8 / *We have breakfast at 8*
Nosotros nos desayunamos a las 8 / *We have breakfast at 8*

Fin del capítulo / *End of chapter*

VII. Adjetivos posesivos / Possessive Adjectives

Quick note: always remember nouns, articles and adjectives in Spanish need to match gender and quantity. This means, translations for words such as "my", "your", "their" will have at least a singular and a plural form.

Adjetivos posesivos
MI / Mis – *My*
Mi casa es bonita – *My house is pretty*
Mis rosas son rojas – *My roses are red*

Tu / Tus – *Your*
Tu país natal es Costa Rica – *Your homeland is Costa Rica*
Tus zapatos son azules – *Your shoes are blue*

Su – Him / her (singular form)
Pedro viven con su perro – *Pedro lives with his dog*
Maria vive con su perro – *Maria lives with her dog*

Sus – him / her (plural form)
Pedro vive con sus perros – *Pedro lives with his dogs*
María vive con sus perros – Maria lives with her dogs

Nuestro / Nuestra – Our (masculine and feminine form)
Nuestro trabajo es muy bueno – *Our job is very good*
Nuestra casa está en la playa – *Our house is in the beach*
Nuestros / Nuestras – Our (plural form masculine and feminine)
Nuestros amigos están en Francia – *Our Friends are in France*
Nuestras clases de español son a las 10:00 – *Our Spanish clases are at 10:00*

Su / Sus – *Their (singular and plural form)*
¿Esta es su casa? – *Is this their house?*
Los libros de sus amigos – *The books of their friends.*

Vocabulario

a. La familia (The family)

Abuelo / Abuela – *Grandfather / Grandmother*
Mamá / Madre – *Mom / Mother*
Papá / Padre – *Dad / Father*
Esposo / Esposa – *Husband / Wife*
Hijo / Hija – Son / Daughter
Hermano / Hermana – Brother / Sister
Nieto / Nieta – *Grandson / Grandaughter*
Tío / Tía – *Uncle / Aunt*
Primo / Prima – *Cousin (masculine and feminine form)*
Sobrino / Sobrina – *Niece (masculine and feminine form)*

Pequeña historia – Short story

Mi pequeña familia – *My small family*

Quiero hablar de mi pequeña familia. Somos solo cuatro personas: mi papá, mi mamá y mi perro, por cierto, no es pequeño, es muy grande y finalmente, yo. – *I want to talk about my little family. We are only four people: my dad, my mom and my dog, by the way, he's not small, is very big and finally, me*

La casa también es pequeña. Tiene dos habitaciones y un baño pequeño. - *The house is also small. It has two bedrooms and a small bathroom.*

Por la mañana, desayunamos juntos en la cocina pequeña. - *In the morning, we have breakfast together in the small kitchen.*

Me gusta desayunar, porque, por las mañanas siempre tengo hambre. - *I like to have breakfast because, in the morning, I am always hungry*

.A mi papá le gusta jugar béisbol con sus amigos y los sábados salir con mi mamá al "Parque Pequeño", se llama así, pero no es pequeño. - *My dad likes to like baseball with his friends and on Saturdays, I go out with my mom to the "Small Park" that's its name, but is not small.*

Como puedes ver, todo es pequeño, en una casa pequeña, una familia pequeña, pero muy feliz – *As you can see, everything is small, a small house, a small family, but very happy*

Fin de la historia – *End of the story*

Vocabulario

b. Paises y nacionalidades (Countries and nationalities)

Algunos países según los continentes (Some countries according to the continents)

América – America
Estados Unidos / *United States*
Canadá
México
Costa Rica
Panamá
Colombia
Venezuela
Perú
Ecuador
Brasil
Argentina
Chile
América del norte / *North America*
América central / *Central America*
América del sur / *South America*

Islas del caribe / Caribbean islands
Cuba
Haití
República Dominicana / *Dominican Republic*
Puerto Rico / *Porto Rico*
Jamaica / *Jamaica*

Europa / Europe
España / *Spain*
Portugal / Portugal
Francia / *France*
Italia / *Italy*
Alemania / *Germany*
Reino Unido / United Kingdom
Inglaterra / *England*
Irlanda / *Ireland*
Escocia / *Scotland*
Rusia / Russia
Unión Europea / *European Union*

Asia / Asia
China
India
Vietnam
Japón
Corea del Norte / *North Korea*
Corea del Sur / *South Korea*
Filipinas / Philippines
Siria
Irak
Turquía

Africa
Libia
Marruecos / *Morocco*
Suráfrica / South Africa
Cabo verde / *Cape*

Camerún
Costa de Marfil / *Ivory coast*
Egipto / *Egypt*
Libia
Madagascar
Zimbabue

Australia / *Australia*
Oceanía

Algunas nacionalidades (Some nationalities)

Quick note: nationalities are considered adjectives as they describe an identity. If we follow the Spanish rule for adjectives, this means we will find 4 translations for every nationality. In other words, *American*, for example, could be translated as americano, americana, americanos and / or americanas, which can be understood as a singular masculine, singular feminine, plural masculine and plural feminine form respectively.

Nacionalidades en América / *Nationalities in America*
Mexicano, Mexicana / *Mexican*
Cubano, Cubana / *Cuban*
Colombiano, Colombiana / *Colombian*
Venezolano, Venezolana / *Venezuelan*
Argentino, Argentina / *Argentinian*
Estadounidense / *American*
Americano, Americana / *American*

Canadiense / *Canadian*

Nacionalidades en Europa / *Nationalities in Europe*
Español, Española / *Spaniard*
Portugués, Portuguesa / *Portuguese*
Francés, Francesa / French
Italiano, Italiana / *Italian*
Inglés, Inglesa / *English*
Británico, Británica / *British*
Alemán, Alemana, / *German*
Ruso, Rusa / *Russian*

Nacionalidades en Asia / *Nationalities in Asia*
Chino, China / *Chinese*
Japonés, Japonesa / *Japanese*
Coreano, Coreana / Korean

Nacionalidades en África / *Nationalities in Africa*
Africano, Africana / *African*

Australiano, Australiana / *Australian*

Practica de conversación – Diálogos (Conversation practice – Dialogues)
1) ¿De dónde eres? – *Where are you from?*
Soy de Canadá ¿y tú? – *I'm from Canada and you?*
Soy de España, pero vivo en Italia – *I'm from Spanish, but I live in Italy*

2) Este año quiero viajar por América Latina – *This year I want to travel around Latin America*
¡Genial! ¿Y qué países piensas visitar? – *Great! And what countries are you planning to visit?*
Quiero conocer Colombia, Perú y Ecuador – *I want to know Colombia, Peru and Ecuador*

3) ¿Qué idiomas hablas? – *What languages do you speak?*
Hablo inglés, francés, español y portugués – *I speak English, French, Spanish and Portuguese*
¿En serio? ¿Y cuál es tu idioma native? – *Really? And what's your native language?*
Español, porque nací en Perú – *Spanish, because I was born in Peru*

4) ¿Dónde naciste? – *Where were you born?*
Nací en Japón pero mis padres son de Estados Unidos – *I was born in Japan but my parents are from United States*
¿Entonces hablas Inglés y Japonés? – *So, do you speak English and Japanese?*
¡Así es! – *That's right*

Fin del diálogo– *End of the diálogo*

Fin del capítulo / *End of chapter*

VIII. Preposiciones – Prepositions

PARTE I - Part one
A – *to*
Hoy voy a la playa – *Today I go to the beach.*

De – *From, Of*
Ella es de Canadá – *She is from Canada*
Estados Unidos de América – *United States of America*

Al – *to the (masculine form)*
Nosotros queremos ir al parque – *We want to go to the park*

Del – *From the, Of the (masculine form)*
Yo vengo del hospital – *I come from the hospital*
Los ejercicios del libro – *The exercises of the book*

Quick note: In Spanish, articles "a" and "de" take a different form *only* when followed by the singular masculine article "el", making "a + el" becomes "al" and "de + el" becomes "del". These are known as contracted articles or *"artículos contractados"*.

Vocabulario

Lugares I (Places I)

El restaurante / *The restaurant*
Todos los días, Juana va al mismo restaurant / *Everyday, Juana goes to the same restaurant*

El hospital / *The hospital*
¿Quieres ir al hospital a ver un doctor? / *Do you want to go to the hospital to see a doctor?*

La playa / *The beach*
Los muchachos van a la playa esta tarde / *The guys go to the beach this afternoon*

El parque / *The park*
Mis hijos van a correr al parque / *My kids are going to run to the park*

El supermercado / *The supermarker*
Necesito comprar comida. Tengo que ir al supermercado / *I need to buy food. I have to go to the supermarket*

La escuela / *The school*
MI mamá va a la escuela de lunes a viernes. Es su trabajo. *My mom goes to school from Monday to Friday. It's her job.*

PARTE II – Part II

En – *In, on, at*

Quick note: In Spanish, these three preposition (in, on, at) can have the same translation no matter the situation in which you need to use it. Everything will be understood following a logical context. If we are talking about a table with no drawers, the most logical position for something to be placed would be *on* the table. In Spanish it will have the same translation "en" but it's understood that the object will be *on* that specific place.

Practica de conversación – Diálogos (Conversation practice – Dialogues)

1) ¿Dónde están las llaves? – *Where are the keys?*
Están en la mesa – *They are on the table*

2) ¿Quieres ir conmigo a una fiesta? – *Do you want to come with me to a party?*
¿Y dónde es? – *And where is it?*
Es en casa de Mario – *It's at Mario's house*

3) Ana, ¿dónde está la pizza? – *Ana, where's the pizza?*
Está en la nevera – *It's in the fridge*

4) ¿Dónde está Alejandro? – *Where's Alejandro?*
A esta hora debe estar en el trabajo – *At this time, he must be at work.*

Fin del diálogo– *End of the diálogo*

PARTE III – *Part III*

Arriba – *Up or upstairs*
Sus amigos están arriba – *You medicines are upstairs*

Abajo – *Down*
El edificio se viene abajo – *The building is coming down.*

Encima – *Above*
Tus medicinas están encima del cajón – *Your medicines are above the drawer.*

Debajo – *Beneath / Debajo*
Debajo de la tierra podemos encontrar minerales – *Beneath the earth, we can find minerals*

Cerca – *Close*
Tu hermano está cerca. *Your brother is close.*

Lejos – *Far*
El restaurante está lejos – *The restaurant is far*

Al lado – *Next to*
Tu casa está al lado de nuestra casa – *Your house is next to our house.*

Al frente – *In front of*
El supermercado está al frente de la escuela – *The supermarket is in front of the school.*

PARTE IV : Part IV

Preposiciones "Por" y "para" – Prepositions "por" and "para"

Quick note: these two prepositions often create confusion during the student's learning process. This is due to their multiple translations in English, which can be often be used even for either "por" or "para" in Spanish.

Preposición "Por" – Preposition "por"
It explains a cause, a beginning, or a period of time.

El atleta corre por el parque – *The athlete runs by the park*
Siempre paso por la avenida azul – *I always pass by the blue avenue*
Veo muchos árboles por esta zona – *I see many trees around this zone*
Él está castigado por estar tarde – *He is grounded because of being late.*
Nosotros vendemos la casa por motivos laborales – *We sell the house due to work reasons.*

Preposición "para" – Preposition "para"
It explains an objective, a goal, the ending or a specific moment.

Ella va para la fiesta – *She goes to the party*
Yo trabajo para ganar dinero – *I work in order to earn money*
Este regale es para Juan – *This gift is for Juan*
Quiero el Proyecto para mañana en la mañana – *I want the project for tomorrow morning*

Pequeña historia – Short story
Para ti y por ti, mi amor – *For you and because of you, my love*

Voy a la tienda por unas flores para ti. - *I go to the store for some flowers for you.*

Para mañana quiero pasear por la playa, yo llevo el bloqueador solar para ti. - *For tomorrow I want to walk by the beach, I'll bring the sunscreen for you*

El año que viene vamos para Argentina porque dices que te gusta ese país. Es un viaje por ti. –*Next year we are going to Argentina because you say you like that country. It's a trip for you.*

Ahora voy a tomar café y salir a comprar unos chocolates, para ti, mi amor - *Now I'm going to drink coffee and go out to buy some chocolates, for you, my love.*

Fin de la historia – *End of the story*

Vocabulario

<u>La casa, El hogar (The house, the home)</u>

La sala - *The living room*
¡Qué bonita sala! – *What a beautiful living room!*

La cocina – *The kitchen*
La cocina está al lado de la sala – *The kitchen is next to the living room*

El comedor – *The dining room*
Es hora de cenar, vamos al comedor – *It's time to have diner, let's go to the dining room*

La habitación – *The bedroom*
¿Cuántas habitaciones tiene tu casa? – *How many bedrooms does your house have?*

El baño – *The bathroom*
Mi casa tiene un baño – *My house has a bathroom*

El piso – *The floor*
¿Cuántos pisos tiene tu casa? – *How many floors does your house have?*

El jardín – *The garden*

Mi lugar favorito de la casa, es el jardín – *My favorite place of the house is the garden.*

El patio – *The backyard*
Los niños juegan en el patio – *The kids play in the backyard*

El sótano – *The basement*
¿Tu casa tiene sótano? – *Does your house have basement?*

La terraza – *The terrace*
Vamos a la terraza esta noche – *Let's go to the terrace tonight*

El ático – *The attic*
El ático está arriba – *The attic is upstairs.*

El garaje – *The garage*
Guardo el carro en el garaje – *I keep the car in the garage*

El mueble – *The sofá*
Tienes unos muebles muy bonitos – *You have some pretty sofás*

La silla – *The chair*
Puedes tomar una silla si quieres – *You can take a chair if you want*

La mesa – *The table*
La mesa tiene flores rojas – *The table has red flowers*

La cama – *The bed*
La cama está cómoda – *The bed is comfortable*

La televisión – *The television*
Todas las tardes mi abuelo mira televisión – *Every afternoon, my granddad watches televisión*

El carro – *The car*
Tengo el carro en el garaje – *I have the car in the garaje*

Fin del capítulo / *End of chapter*

IX. Los números y la fecha / The numbers and the date

1. Los números (Numbers)

Uno - *One*
Dos - *Two*
Tres - *Three*
Cuatro - *Four*
Cinco - Five
Seis - *Six*
Siete - Seven
Ocho - *Eight*
Nueve - *Nine*
Diez - *Ten*
Once - *Eleven*
Doce - *Twelve*
Trece - *Thirteen*
Catorce - *Fourteen*
Quince - *Fifteen*
Dieciseis - *Sixteen*
Diecisiete - *Seventeen*
Dieciocho – *Eighteen*
Diecinueve - *Nineteen*
Veinte - *Twenty*
Treinta - *Thirty*

Cuarenta – *Forty*
Cincuenta - *Fifty*
Sesenta - *Sixty*
Setenta - *Seventy*
Ochenta – *Eighty*
Noventa - *Ninety*
Cien – *One hundred*
Mil – *One thousand*
Millón – *One million*

2. Los días de la semana (The days of the week)

Lunes – *Monday*
Martes – *Tuesday*
Miércoles – *Wednesday*
Jueves – *Thursday*
Viernes – *Friday*
Sábado – *Saturday*
Domingo – *Sunday*
Fines de semana - *Weekends*

Practica de conversación – Diálogos (Conversation practice – Dialogues)

1) ¿Tú trabajas de lunes a viernes? – *Do you work from Monday to Friday?*
Si, y a veces los sábados si me necesitan – *I do, and also on Saturdays if they need me*

2) Normalmente voy a la playa los fines de semana ¿y tú? – *I normally go to the beach on weekends, and you?*

Pues, normalmente los fines de semana me quedo en mi casa – *Well, normally on weekends I stay in my house*

3) Yo tengo que ir a la escuela todos los días. ¡Qué fastidio! – *I have to go to school every day. How annoying!*
Pero la escuela es divertida – *But school is fun.*
No lo creo – *I don't think so.*

4) ¿Cuándo tienes clases de español? – *When do you have Spanish classes?*
Tengo español los lunes, miércoles y viernes – *I have Spanish on Mondays, Wednesdays and Fridays*

Fin del diálogo – *End of the diálogo*

---

3. Meses del año

Enero – *January*
Yo nací el 30 de enero de 1994 / *I was born in January 30, 1994*

Febrero – *February*
Mi hermana nació en febrero / *My sister was born in February*

Marzo – *March*
En marzo celebramos el día de la independencia / *On Mars, we celebrate the day of the Independence*

Abril – *April*
Nos vamos de viaje el 14 de abril / We are going to travel on April 14

Mayo – *May*
Mayo es el mes de las madres / *May is mothers' month*

Junio – *June*
Tú naciste el 3 de Junio de 2002 / *You were born on June 3rd, 2002*

Julio – *July*
Julio es mi mes favorite / *July is my favorite month*

Agosto – *August*
Mi graduación es en Agosto / *My graduation is in August*

Septiembre – *September*
Su cumpleaños es en septiembre / *His birthday is in September*

Octubre – *October*
Ella quiere ir a España en octubre / *She wants to go to Spain in October*

Noviembre – *November*
Juan nació el 20 de noviembre / *Juan was born on November 20*

Deciembre – *December*

Nosotros no celebramos navidad en diciembre / *We don't celebrate christmas in December*

Fin del capítulo / *End of chapter*

X. Adjetivos demostrativos / Demonstrative adjectives

Este – *This (singular masculine form)*
Este perro es hermoso – *This dog is beautiful*

Esta – *This (singular feminine form)*
Esta comida está deliciosa – *This food is delicious*

Estos – *These (plural masculine form)*
Estos zapatos son azules – *These shoes are blue*

Estas – *These (plural feminine form)*
Estas casas son grandes – *These houses are big*

Aquel, Aquella – *That (for longer distances. Singular masculine and feminine form)*
Vamos a aquel centro comercial – *We go to that mall over there.*
Mi mamá es dueña de aquella casa en la montaña – *My mom is the owner of that house over there in the mountain.*

Aquellos, Aquellas – *Those (for longer distances. Plural masculine and feminine form)*

Aquellos días quedaron en el pasado – *Those days remained in the past*
Aquellas chicas cerca de la barra, son mis amigas – *Those girls over there in the bar, are my friends.*

Vocabulario
Ropa y accesorios (Clothes)

La camisa / *Shirt*
Me gusta esta camisa – *I like this shirt*

EL pantalón / *Pants*
Ponte estos pantalones – *Put on these pants*

La popa interior / *Underwear*
Necesito comprar ropa interior nueva – *I need to buy new underwear*

Los zapatos / *Shoes*
¿Cuáles zapatos quieres? ¿Aquellos? – *Which shoes do you want? Those over there?*

Las sandalias / *Sandals*
Recuerda llevar sandalias para la plata – *Remember to bring some sandals to the beach*

Las medias / *Socks*
Hace mucho frío, necesito un par de medias – *It's very cold, I need a pair of socks*

El suéter / *Sweater*
Si vamos a salir, lleva un suéter – *If we are going out, bring a sweater*

La gorra / *Cap*
Me gusta esa gorra roja – *I like that red cap*

El short / *Short*
Mira ese short – *Look at that short*

Los tacones / *Heels*
Esos tacones son muy bonitos – *Those heles are very pretty*

Aparatos electrónicos (Electronic devices)

El teléfono – *Phone*
El teléfono celular – *Cell pone*
La lavadora – *Washing machine*
La nevera – *Fridge*
La computadora – *Computer or desktop*
La laptop – *Laptop*
El televisor, la televisión – Television

Practica de conversación – Diálogos (Conversation practice – Dialogues)

1) ¿Conoces un sitio donde puedo comprar un buen televisor? – *Do you know a place where I can buy a good television?*

Creo que hay un sitio cerca de mi casa – *I think there's a good place near my house*

2) No puedo estudiar – *I can't study*
¿Por qué? – *Why?*
Mi computadora no funciona – *My computer doesn't work*

3) Mira este nuevo teléfono – *look at this new phone*
Es verdad, está muy bonito – *It's true, it's beautiful*

Fin del diálogo– *End of the diálogo*

Fin del capítulo / *End of chapter*

XI. Verbo "Gustar" / Verb "to like"

Quick note: In Spanish, "to like" works in a different way compared to English, but also compared to other verbs we have learned during the book. "Gustar" uses a pronoun called "object pronoun" and this will be placed before the conjugation of the verb. Also, this verb is usually conjugated in two forms, singular "gusta" (when someone likes one thing) and plural "gustan" (when someone likes more than one thing)

Conjugación / *Conjugation*
Me gusta, Me gustan – *I like*
Me gusta la pizza – *I like pizza*

Te gusta, Te gustan – *You like*
Me gustan los deportes extremos – *I like extreme sports*

Le gusta, Le gustan – *He or She likes*
A María le gustan las fiestas – *Maria likes parties*
A José no le gusta beber café – *Jose doesn't like to drink coffee*

Nos gusta, Nos gustan – *We like*
Los fines de semana nos gusta ir a la playa – *On weekends, we like to go to the beach*

Les gusta, Les gustan – They like
A ellos no les gusta la comida italiana – *They don't like italian food*

Vocabulario
<u>La comida I (The food I)</u>

Vegetales – *Vegetables*
Tomate – *Tomato*
Papa – *Potato*
Cebolla – *Onion*
Carne – *Meat*
Pollo – *Chicken*
Pescado – *Fish*
Arroz – *Rice*
Pasta
Queso – *Cheese*
Jamón – *Jam*
Huevos – *Eggs*
Pan - *Bread*
Frutas – *Fruits*
Manzana – *Apple*
Pera – *Pear*
Naranja – *Orange*
Banana
Piña – *Pineapple*

Sandía – *Watermelon*
Melón – *Melon*
Papaya
Ingredientes – *Ingredients*
Sal – *Salt*
Azucar – *Sugar*
Mantequilla - *Butter*
Pimienta – *Pepper*

Práctica de conversación – Diálogos – Conversation practice – Dialogues

1) Carlos, ¿me puedes decir qué necesito para preparar la sopa? – *Carlos, can you tell me what do I need to prepare the soup?*
Necesitamos mucho ajo, vegetales y la carne – *We need a lot of garlic, vegetables and the meat*

2) ¿Tú eres vegetariano? – *Are you vegetarian?*
Sí, aunque a veces como pollo – *I am, but sometimes I eat chicken*

3) ¿Cuál es tu comida favorita? – *What's your favorite food?*
Adivina, soy italiano – *Guess what, I'm italian.*

Fin del diálogo– *End of the diálogo*

Vocabulario

Pasatiempos / Hobbies

La natación / *Swimming*
Escuchar música / *Listening to music*
Leer, la lectura / *Reading*
Escribir, la escritura / *Writing*
Hacer ejercicio / *Doing exercise*
Cantar / *Singing*
Practicar, La práctica / *Practicing*
Cocinar, La cocina / *Cooking*
Bailar, El baile / *Dancing*
Fumar / *Smoking*
Tocar instrumentos / *Playing instruments*

Practica de conversación – Diálogos (Conversation practice – Dialogues)

1) ¿Cuál es tu actividad favorita? – *What's your favorite activity?*
Me gusta mucho la natación – *I like swimming very much*

2) La lectura es mi pasión – *Reading is my passion*
¿Y no te gusta escribir? – *And you don't like writing?*
Hm, no mucho – *Hm, not a lot.*

3) Los doctores dicen que fumar es malo para la salud – *Doctors say smoking is bad for health.*
Sí, lo sé – *Yes, I know*

4) A mí hijo le encanta tocar instrumentos. Quiere ser artista – *My son loves playing instruments. He wants to be an artist.*

5) En América Latina, bailar es una actividad popular / *In Latin america, dancing is a popular activity.*

Fin del diálogo– *End of the diálogo*

Fin del capítulo / *End of chapter*

XII. Comparaciones / Comparisons

Introduction: In Spanish, creating comparative sentences such as "He is taller than her" work in a different way. In English, most of the adjectives have to be modified in these kind of sentences, so tall becomes taller, big becomes bigger and so on. In Spanish, this rule doesn't apply and they will all have this structure "más alto", "más grande", as if you are literally saying "more tall" or "more big" respectively. The same will happen will superlative comparisons, for example: I am the tallest. Let's begin. *Vamos a comenzar.*

Oraciones comparativas / Comparative sentences

Quick note: remember adjectives in Spanish need to always match gender and quantity.

Más alto, Más alta / *Taller (masculine and feminine form)*
Juan es más alto es Pedro / *Juan is taller tan Pedro*
María es más grande que Ana / *Maria is taller than Ana*

Más pequeño, Más pequeña / *Smaller (masculine and feminine form)*

Uruguay es más pequeño que Argentina / *Uruguay is smaller than Argentina*

Más inteligente / *More intelligent (both masculine and feminine form)*
Juan y Ana son más inteligentes que Pedro y María / *Juan and Ana are more intelligent than Pedro and Maria*

Mejor / *Better*
El arroz es mejor que la pasta / *Rice is better than pasta*

Peor / *Worse*
Esta película es peor que el libro / *This movie is worse than the book*

Oraciones superlativas / Superlative sentences

El más alto, La más alta / *The tallest (masculine and feminine form)*
Juan es el más alto de la clase / *Juan is the talles in the classroom*

El más grande, La más grande / *The biggest (masculine and feminine form)*
Rusia es el país más grande del mundo / *Russia is the biggest country in the world*

El más bonito, La más bonita / *The prettiest (masculine and feminine form)*

Esta es la ciudad más bonita de todas / *This is the prettiest cities of all.*

El mejor, La mejor / *The best (masculine and feminine)*
Esta playa es la mejor / *This beach is the best*
Este libro es el mejor / *This book is the best*

El peor, La peor / *The worst (masculine and feminine)*
Esta película es la peor / *This film is the worst*
Esos chicos son los peores / *Those guys are the worst.*

Comparaciones de igualdad / *Comparisons of equality*

Quick note: In English, an example of these sentences is: She is as good as María.
In Spanish, we need two different words to translate both "as" in the previous sentence. These words are "*tan*" and "*como*".
Ejemplos / *Examples*:

Ella es tan buena como María / *She is as good as María*

Dicen que la soya es tan nutritiva como la carne / *They say soy is as nutritive as meat*

Yo soy tan alto como mi hermano / *I'm as tall as my brother*

Esa película es tan mala como el libro / *That movie is as bad as the book*

Vocabulario
Medios de transporte (Ways of transportation)

El metro / *Metro, subway*
Para regresar a casa, siempre tomo el metro porque es más rápido que el bus / To get back home, I have to take the metro because is faster than the bus

El tren / *Train*
El Maglev es el tren más rápido del mundo / The Maglev is the fastest train in the world

El avión / *Plane*
El avión sale a las 10:30 mañana / The plane leaves tomorrow at 10:30

El barco / *Ship*
Ana me dijo que viajar en barco es mejor que en avión / *Ana told me that travelling by ship is better than by plain*

El bus / *Bus*
¿Dónde puedo tomar el bus principal? / *Where can I take the main bus?*

El taxi / *Taxi*
Esta compañía de taxi es tan buena como la de mi ciudad / *This taxi company is as good as the one from my city.*

La moto / *Bike*
Mañana me compro la moto que me gusta / *Tomorrow I buy the bike that I like*

La bicicleta / *Bicycle*
Mi bicicleta es tan bonita como la tuya / *My bicycle is as pretty as yours.*

A pie / *On foot*
Yo siempre voy a pie de mi casa a la oficina / *I always go on foot from my house to the office*

Fin del capítulo / *End of chapter*

XIII. Adverbios / Adverbs

Adverbios de tiempo / Adverbs of time

Ayer / *Yesterday*
Ayer hablé con Juan / *Yesterday I talked to Juan*

Hoy / *Today*
¿Qué día es hoy? / *What day is today?*

Mañana / *Tomorrow*
¿Que vamos a hacer mañana? / *What are we going to do tomorrow?*

Esta noche / *Tonight*
La fiesta es esta noche / *The party is tonight*

Pronto / *Soon*
Es demasiado pronto / *it's too soon*

Tarde / *Late*
Creo que manuel llega tarde hoy / *I think Manuel arrives late today*

Temprano / *Early*
¿No es muy temprano para almorzar? / *isn't it too early to have lunch?*

Adverbios de frecuencia

Interesting fact: most of the words ending with "-ly" in English, i.e. "Totally", will most likely have a similar version in Spanish and these last two letter "-ly" will be translated as "mente". *Vamos a los ejemplos.* Let's go to the examples

Siempre / *Always*
Yo siempre practico español / *I always practice Spanish*

Usualmente / *Usually*
Usualmente, Maria va a la playa / *Usually, Maria goes to the beach*

Normalmente, generalmente / *Normally, Generally*
Generalmente los niños comienzan a hablar al primer año. *Generally, kids start speaking at the first year.*

A menudo / *Often*
A menudo visito a mi familia en México / *I often visit my family in Mexico*

A veces / *Sometimes*
A veces tomo café en la mañana / *Sometimes I drink coffee in the morning*
Nunca / *Never*
Él nunca hace la tarea / *He never does homework*

Adverbios de lugar / *Adverbs of place*

Aquí / *Here*
La clase es aquí en este salón / *The house is here in this classroom*

Allá / *There*
El chico quiere ir allá / *The kid wants to go there*

Cerca / *Near*
¿La estación del metro está cerca? / *Is the train station close?*

Lejos / *Far*
Su familia se fue muy lejos / *His family went out very far*

Adverbios de modo / *Adverbs of manner*

Fácilmente / Easily
Él habla español fácilmente / He easily speaks Spanish

Difícilmente / *Hardly*
Dificilmente creo que pueda venir / *I hardly think he can come*

Rápidamente / *Quickly, Fastly*
El atleta llega a la meta rápidamente / *The athlete gets to the goal quickly*

Slowly / *Lentamente*

La tortuga camina muy lentamente / *The turtle walks very slowly*
Básicamente / *Basically*
Básicamente, un adverbio describe una acción / *Basically, an adverbs describes an action*

Adverbios de aproximación
Casi / *Almost*
Esta mañana casi llego tarde al trabajo / *This morning, I almost got late to work*
Ella es casi tan inteligente como María / *She is almost as smart as Maria*

Apenas / *Barely*
Hoy apenas es miércoles / *Today is barley Wednesday*

Prácticamente / *Practically*
El concierto estuvo prácticamente bueno / *The concert was practically good.*

Vocabulario
Animales / Animals

Quick note: Grammatically, animals are nouns, and, in Spanish, remember most of the nouns will have a masculine and a feminine form.

Animales del bosque y la jungla / Animals of the forest and jungle

Mono, mona / *Monkey*
Tigre / Tigresa / *Tiger*
León, Leona / *Lion*
Rana / *Frog*
Sapo / *Toad*
Ave, pájaro / *Bird*
Pez / *Fish*
Hormiga / *Ant*
Araña / *Spider*

Animales del desierto / Animals of the desert

Elefante / *Elephant*
Zebra / *Zebra*
Camello / *Camel*
Serpiente / *Snake*
Escorpión / *Scorpio*

Animales domésticos y de granja / Domestic and farm animals

Perro, perra / *Dog*
Gato, gata / *Cat*
Gallo / *Rooster*
Gallina / Hen
Pollo / Chicken
Vaca / *Cow*

Toro / *Bull*
Caballo / *Horse*
Cerdo / *Pig*
Oveja / *Sheep*

Especies / Species

Reptiles / *Reptiles*
Mamíferos / *Mammals*
Insectos / *Insects*

Pequeña historia – Short story
El debate / ***The debate***

En una granja se realiza un debate sobre un tema muy controversial: ¿Quién es primero? ¿El huevo o la gallina? El cerdo es el primero en hablar: / *In a farm, there is a debate about a very controversial topic: Who is the first? The egg or the chicken? The pig is the first to speak:*

Pues a mí me parece compañeros, que el huevo es primero - *well it seems to me pals, that the egg is the first.*

Luego la oveja dice – *Then the sheep says*

El amigo cerdo tiene razón, básicamente una gallina no viene de otro lado. El primer paso es el huevo – *Friend pig is right, basically, a chicken doesn't come from any other place. The first step is the egg*

Luego el sabio búho tranquilamente dice – *Then the wise owl calmly says:*

¡Silencio! Están equivocados. No es el huevo, y tampoco es la gallina. Primero soy yo. - *Silence! You are all wrong, it's not the egg and it's not the chicken either. The first one is me.*

Luego el caballo grita y dice – *Then the horse yells and says*

¡este chico está loco! Obviamente primero es el caballo. Nosotros somos rápidos y siempre somos los primeros en llegar a la meta. – *This guy is crazy! Obviously the first one is the horse. We are fast and we are always the first to get to the goal.*

Y finalmente la gallina dice – *And finally the chicken says*

La Gallina: yo no sé quién es primero, pero yo opino que tiene que ser el gallo porque él es el amor de mi vida. *I don't know who's first but I think it has to be the rooster because he's the love of my life.*
Fin de la historia – *End of the story*

Fin del capítulo / *End of chapter*

XIV. Tiempo presente continuo / Present continuous tense

Introduction: In Spanish, the structure of the present continuous tense is similar to English. To create this tense you need a noun, the verb *"estar"* conjugated in the present tense, and the gerund. In Spanish, there are only two ways of translating the "-ing" from English, these are *"=ando"* for all the verbs ending in *"-ar"* and *"-iendo"* for the verbs ending in either *"-er"* or *"-ir"*. *Vamos a los ejemplos* / let's go to the examples.

Bailar, Bailando / *To dance, Dancing*
María está bailando salsa muy bien / *Maria is dancing salsa very well*

Escuchar, Escuchando / *To listen, Listening*
Tú estás escuchando oraciones en español / *You are listening to sentences in Spanish*

Aprender, Aprendiendo / *To learn, Learning*
Estamos aprendiendo presente continuo / *We are learning the present continuous*

Leer, Leyendo / *To read, Reading*
El chico está leyendo el texto / *The guy is reading the text*

Vivir, Viviendo / *To live, Living*
Mi amiga está viviendo en Honduras / *My friend is living in Honduras*

Escribir, Escribiendo / *To write, Writing*
El autor está escribiendo este libro / *The author is writing this book*

Quick note: In Spanish, the gerund is used only to create the present continuous tense, therefore, activities or hobbies such as swimming will not be translated as *"nadando"*, on the contrary, activities like these will have a different translation such as *"nadar"* or *"natación"* In other words, gerund in Spanish is never used as a noun but as a verb. You can go back to Chapter IX and review the vocabulary about hobbies.

Practica de conversación – Diálogos (Conversation practice – Dialogues)

1) ¿Qué estás haciendo? – *What are you doing?*
Estoy comprando cosas en el Mercado – *I'm buying stuffs in the market.*

2) ¿Por qué estás llorando? – *Why are you crying?*
Porque estoy muy triste – *Because I'm very sad*

3) Wow, qué bien hablas español – *Wow, how well you speak Spanish*
Sí, estoy practicando todos los días – *Yes, I'm practicing every day*

4) ¿Desde qué hora están trabajando? – *From what time are you working?*
Estamos trabajando desde las 8:00 hasta las 5:00 – *We are working from 8:00 until 5:00*

Fin del diálogo– *End of the diálogo*

Vocabulario

<u>Lugares II (Places II)</u>
La plaza / *Square*
Los niños están jugando en la plaza / *The kids are playing at the square*

La universidad / *University*
Estoy estudiando en la universidad de Chile / *I'm studying in the university of Chile*

Centro comercial / *Mall*
Mi esposa está comprando ropa en el centro comercial / *My wife is buying clothes at the mall*

Tienda / *Store*
Estamos viviendo cerca de la tienda / *We are living close to the store*

Aeropuerto / *Airport*
El avión está llegando al aeropuerto / *The plane is arriving at the airport*

El centro de la ciudad / *The city center*
Ahora estamos caminando por el centro de la ciudad / *Now we are walking by the center of the city*

La calle / *The Street*
Estoy conduciendo por la calle Salazar / *I'm driving by the Salazar Street.*

La avenida / *The avenue*
Está pasando algo en la avenida / *Something is happening in the avenue*

Profesiones II (Professions II)

Policia / *Police or pólice officer*
Juan está trabajando como policía en su ciudad / *Juan is working as a police officer in his city*

Bombero / *Fireman*
Los bomberos están ayudando a la gente a escapar / *The firemen are helping the people to escape*

Tenista / *Tennis player*
Este tenista está ganando siempre / *This tennis player is always winning*

Futbolista / Football or soccer player
Los futbolistas están haciendo un gran trabajo / *The football player are doing a great job*

Beisbolista / *Baseball player*
El beisbolista está bateando como un pro / *The baseball player is hitting like a pro*

Enfermero, Enfermera / *Nurse*
La enfermera está salvando al paciente / *The nurse is saving the patient*

Arquitecto, Arquitecta / *Architect*
Mi amigo es arquitecto y está diseñando un edificio nuevo / *My friend is an architect and she's designing a new building*

Científico / *Scientist*
Los científicos están intentando encontrar la vacuna / *The scientists are trying to find the vaccine*

Sociólogo, socióloga / *Sociologist*
Este es un reconocido sociólogo. Está escribiendo un libro sobre la cultura actual / *This is a well-known sociologist. He is writing a book about current culture*

Físico / *Physicist*
Este físico está creando una nueva teoría / *This physicist is creating a new theory*

Dentista / *Dentist*
Maria está estudiando para ser dentista / *Maria is studying to become a dentist*

La naturaleza (Nature)

La montaña / *The mountain*
Los chicos están yendo a la montaña / *The guys are going to the mountain*

El lago / *The lake*
Están contaminando el lago de mi ciudad / *They are polluting the lake of my city*

La laguna / *The lagoon*
En la laguna están cazando patos / *At the lagoon, people are hunting ducks*

La cueva / The cave
Los murciélagos están saliendo de la cueva / The bats are coming out of the cave

La colina / *The hill*
Los escaladores están subiendo la colina / *The hikers are going up the hill*

La arena / *The sand*
Los cangrejos están caminando en la arena / *The crabs are walking on the sand*

El agua / The water
Los peces están nadando en el agua / *The fish are swimming in the wáter*

El fuego / *The fire*
El fuego está quemando la casa / *The fire is burning the house*

El viente / The wind
Este barco está navegando gracias al viento / This ship is sailing thanks to the wind

La tormenta / *The storm*
La tomenta está causando un desastre / *The storm is causing a disaster*

El volcán / *The volcano*
El volcán está erupcionando / *The volcano is erupting*

El tornado / The tornado
¡Cuidado! El tornado se está acercando / *Watch out! The tornado is getting closer*

El clima

Llover / To rain
La lluvia / The rain

Nevar / To snow
La nieve / The snow

Hace calor / It's hot
El calor / *The heat*

Hace frío / It's cold
El frío / The cold

Practica de conversación – Diálogos (Conversation practice – Dialogues)

1) ¿Por qué hace tanto calor? – *Why is it so cold?*
Es porque el aire acondicionado no está funcionando – *It's because the air conditioner isn't working*

2) Mira mamá – *Look mom*
¿Qué? – *What?*
¡Está nevando! – *It's snowing!*

3) ¿Cómo está el clima en Argentina? – *How's the weather in Argentina?*
Últimamente está haciendo mucho frío aquí – It's been getting really cold in here lately

Fin del diálogo– *End of the diálogo*

XV. Pronombres personales tónicos / Tonic personal pronouns

Introduction: in Spanish, personal pronouns have two categories: tonic and atonic pronouns. You already know some tonic pronouns since "yo, tú, él / ella, nosotros..." all of these belong to this category. However, this list is just a bit larger than the words you already know.
Vamos a comenzar / *Let's begin*

Mí ; Conmigo / *Me ; With me*

Esa carta es para mí ¿verdad? / *That letter is for me, right?*
¿Vas al cine conmigo hoy? / *Are you going to the movies with me today?*

Ti ; Contigo / *You ; with you*
Tengo un regalo para ti / *I have a gift for you*
Quiero salir contigo esta noche / *I want to go out with you tonight*

Quick note: these new words only exist for pronuns "me" or "with me" and "you" or "with you" as the plural versions, i.e. "us" or "for us" and "then" or "for them" will not have different versions. This also happens with "her" or "for her". Vamos a continuar / *Let's continue*

Él, Ella ; con él con ella / *HIm, Her ; with him, with her*
Maria no quiere ir con ella / *Maria doesn't want to go with her*
Este pantalón es para ella / *These pants are for her*

Nosotros ; con nosotros / *Us ; with us*
¿Vienes con nosotros a la playa? / *Are you coming with us to the beach?*
Las hamburguesas son para nosotros / *The burgers are for us*

Quick note: Last detail is that these pronouns can be placed at the beginning or at the end of a sentence, BUT they always need or will be preceeded by a preposition and never by a verb. This means that a sentence like "It was me" or "It's you" won't use use a tonic pronoun. *Vamos a los ejemplos* / Let's go to the examples

¿Quién hizo este desastre? ¿Fuiste tú? / *Who did this disaster? Was it you?*

Hola, soy yo, Daniel. ¿No me recuerdas? / *Hey it's me, Daniel. Don't you remember me?*

Vocabulario / *Vocabulary*

Finanzas / *Financee*
Tengo serios problemas con mis finanzas / *I have serious problems with my finances.*

Dinero / *Money*
No tengo dinero para salir a cenar con ella / *I don't have money to go out to dinner with her*

Efectivo / *Cash*
Necesito efectivo para pagar el taxi / *I need cash to pay the taxi.*

Tarjeta de crédito / *Credit Card*
Estoy usando mi tarjeta de crédito para pagar los boletos para nosotros / *I am using my credit card to pay the tickets for us.*

Moneda / *Coin ; Currency*
Esta moneda es para ti / *This coin is for you.*
La moneda de España es el euro / *The currency in Spain is the euro*

Centavos / *Cent*
El boleto de autobús cuesta cincuenta centavos / *The bus ticket costs fifty cents.*

Dólar / *Dollar*

La hamburguesa con queso cuesta un dólar en esa cafetería / *The Cheeseburger costs a dollar at that coffe shop.*

Billete / *Bill*
Tengo un billete de cien dólares para salir con él esta noche / *I have a hundred dollar bill to go out with him*

Cajero automático / *ATM*
El cajero automático del supermercado no funciona / *The supermaket ATM does not work.*

Banco / *Bank*
Voy al banco a retirar dinero para ustedes / *I'm going to the bank to withdraw some money for you guys*

Cheque / *Check*
Necesito un bolígrafo azul para hacer el cheque / *I need a blue pen to write the check.*

Pago / *Pay*
Yo pago el pastel y tú pagas la pizza / *I pay for the cake and you pay for the pizza.*

Cuenta / *Account*
Mi cuenta bancaria está bloqueada de nuevo / *My bank account is blocked again.*

Cuenta / *Check*
La cuenta es para él / *The check is for him.*

Propina / *Tip*
En mi negocio no acepto propina / *I do not accept a tip in my business.*

Caro / *Expensive*
Este es el café más caro de Colombia / *This is the most expensive coffee in Colombia.*

Barato / *Cheap*
En Nueva York nada es barato / *In New York nothing is cheap.*

Gratis / *Free*
Las bebidas son gratis para ustedes / *Drinks are free for you guys*

Descuento / *Discount*
El descuento es solo por hoy / *The discount is only for today.*

Rico / *Rich*
Ese hombre es rico pero no le gusta la comida cara / *That man is rich, but he does not like expensive food.*

Pobre / *Poor*
La gente pobre tiene pocas posibilidades en esta ciudad / *Poor people have little chances in this city.*

Millonario / *Millionaire*

Quiero ser millonario, pero no me gusta trabajar / I want to be a millionaire, but I don't like to work.

Cambio – Vuelto / *Change*
Estoy esperando por mi cambio / *I am waiting for my change.*

Ahorro / *Saving*
El ahorro es la mejor opción para el futuro en este país / *Saving is the best option for the future in this country.*

Practica de Conversación / *Conversation practice*
Disculpe, ¿cuánto cuesta esta camisa? / *Excuse me, how much does this shirt cost?*
Esa camisa cuesta diez dólares / *That shirt costs ten dollars.*
Me gusta, es muy linda y barata, ¿acepta tarjeta de crédito? / *I like it, it is very cute and cheap, do you accept credit card?*
Lo siento. Solo acepto efectivo y cheques / *I am sorry, I only accept cash and checks.*
Tengo un billete de cien dólares, ¿tiene cambio? / *I have a hundred dollar bill. Do you have change?*
Sí, por supuesto / *Yes, of course.*

Fin de la conversación / *End of conversation*

Partes del cuerpo / *Body Parts*

Ojos / *Eyes*
Mi hermana tiene ojos verdes / My sister has green eyes.

Naríz / *Nose*
Mi nariz es demasiado grande / *My nose is too big.*

Boca / *Mouth*
El virus entra por la boca / *The virus enters through the mouth.*

Cara / *Face*
Tu cara está roja / *Your face is red.*

Dientes / *Teeth*
Mi abuela no tiene dientes / *My grandmother has no teeth.*

Brazo / *Arm*
Yo tengo un tatuaje en el brazo / *I have a tattoo on my arm.*

Pierna / *Leg*
Mi pierna izquierda es más larga / *My left leg is longer.*

Enfermedades / *Diseases*

Dolor de Cabeza / *Headache*
No tengo analgésicos para el dolor de cabeza ¿puedes comprar unos por mí? / *I don't have painkillers for the headache, can you buy some for me?*

Cold / *Cold*
Mi paraguas está roto, ahora tengo un resfriado. / *My umbrela is broken, now I have a cold.*

Fiebre / *Fever*
La fiebre es el primer síntoma de la enfermedad. / *Fever is the first Symptom of the disease.*

Tos / *Cough*
Esa tos no se oye bien / *that cough doesn't sound good.*

Dolor / *Pain*
El dolor viene y va / *Pain comes and goes.*

Dolor de garganta / *Sore Throat*
El humo del cigarillo me produce dolor de garganta / *Cigarette smoke gives me a sore throat.*

Dolor de estómago / *Stomach Ache*
Toma, para ti, para tu dolor de estómago. / *Take, for you, for your stomachache*

Practica de Conversación / *Conversation practice*
¿Estás enfermo? No te ves bien. – Are you sick? You don't look well.
No me siento bien, me duelen los brazos y las piernas – *i don't feel good, my arms and legs hurt.*
Tus ojos y nariz están rojos, necesitas ir al hospital - *Your eyes and nose are red, you need to go to the hospital.*

Sí, también me duele la cabeza. – *Yes, my head aches too.*
¿Desde cuando tienes esos síntomas? – *Since when do you have those symptoms?*
No lo sé, pero ahora siento mucho dolor en el estomago, llama una ambulancia – *I don't know, but now I feel a lot of pain in my stomach, call an ambulance.*

Medios de comunicación / *Media*
Carta / *Letter*
No sé cómo abrir esta carta / *I don't know how to open this letter.*

Teléfono / *Phone*
El teléfono no funciona cuando llueve / *The phone doesn't work when it rains.*

Fax / *Fax*
El fax es demasiado viejo, no sé cómo funciona / *The fax is too old, i don't know how does it work.*

Computadora / *Computer*
Esta computora es para ti. Por tu cumpleaños / *This computer is for you. Because of your birthday*

Internet / *Internet*
El servicio de internet es muy caro en mi país / *Internet service is very expensive in my country.*

Radio / *Radio*
Mi mamá escucha la radio en el carro todas las mañanas / *My mom listens to the radio in the car every morning.*

Televisión / *TV*
Yo no veo televisión, prefiero leer libros / *I don't watch TV, I prefer to read books.*

Periódico / Newspaper
Yo compro el periódico todos los domingos / *I buy the newspaper every Sunday.*

Correo postal / *Post mail*
El correo postal es una institución muy importante en los Estados Unidos / *Postal mail is a very important institution in the United States.*

Correo electrónico / *Email*
*No recuerdo la contrase*ña de mi correo electrónico / *I don't remember my email password.*

Sitio web / *Website*
En el sitio web de la empresa está toda la información / *All the information is on the school website.*

Mensaje / *Message*
Mi canción favorita es "Mensaje en una botella" / *My favorite song is "Message in a bottle."*

Anuncio / *Ad*

Odio el anuncio de ese restaurante / *I hate the ad for that restaurant.*

Invitación / *Invitation*
No hay ninguna invitación adentro del buzón / *There is no invitation inside the mailbox.*

Lenguaje de señas / *Sign language*
Estoy aprendiendo lenguaje de señas por internet / *I am learning sing language online.*

XVI. Tiempo Pasado Simple / Simple Past Tense.

Introduction: The simple past tense in Spanish is used to describe actions or events that began and concluded in the past. It is also used to talk about a past action that interrupted or was executed right after another consecutively, i.e "I ate and then I went to sleep". This is critical to keep in mind during your learning journey as in Spanish, past tenses are very specific depeding on how the action happened in a timeline.

As you have learned throughout the book, tenses have different conjugations for every group of verbs, which means you have to always learn the forms you need to apply depending on the tense and the verb group.

Conjugación del verbo "-ar" / *Conjugation of the verb "-ar"*

Comprar / *to buy.*
Yo compré / *I bought*
Compré unos nuevos zapatos, son muy cómodos / *I bought some new shoes, they are very confortable.*

Tú compraste / *You bought*
Tú compraste la cena y yo las bebidas / *You bought dinner and I bought drinks.*

Él / Ella compró / *He / She bought*
Él compró este hermoso anillo / *He bought me this beautiful ring.*
Ella compró los regalos para los niños / *she bought the gifts for the children.*

Nosotros compramos / *We bought*
Nosotros compramos la casa, es muy espaciosa / *We bought the house, is very roomy.*

Ustedes compraron / *You (plural) bought*
Ustedes compraron un auto nuevo / *You guys bought a new car*

Ellos compraron / *They bought*
Ellos compraron un apartamento, tiene una linda vista / *They bought an apartment, it has a nice view.*

Conjugación del verbo "-er" / Conjugation of the verb "-er"

Beber / *to drink.*
Yo bebí de más en la fiesta de anoche / *I drank too much last night.*

Tú bebiste sólo gaseosa anoche / *You drank only soda last night.*

Él bebió jugo y ella cerveza / *He drank juice and she drank beer.*

Nosotros bebimos un vino azul / *We drank a blue wine.*

Ustedes bebieron café esta mañana / *You guys drank coffee this morning*

Ellos bebieron un café frio espumoso / *They drank a cold frothy coffee.*

Conjugación del verbo "-ir" / Conjugation of the verb "-ir"

Vivir / *To live.*

Yo viví en Nueva York por dos años / *I lived in New York for two years.*

Tú viviste con tus abuelos de niño / *You lived with your grandparents as a child.*

Él vivió en un apartamento y ella en una casa / *He lived in an apartment and she lived in a house.*

Nosotros vivíamos cerca del mar / *We lived near the sea.*

¿Ustedes vivieron en México? / *Did you guys live in Mexico?*

Ellos vivieron a las afueras de la ciudad / They lived on the outskirts of the city.

Pequeña historia / *Short story.*

"La carta" / "*The letter*"

Juan recibió una carta de su prometida / *Juan received a letter from his fiancee.*

Así que le escribió una carta de vuelta, la metió en un sobre color rosa con fragancia a fresas y la envío por correo / *So he wrote her a letter back, put it in a pink envelope with strawberry scent and mailed it.*

Se fue ilusionado a su restaurante favorito y pidió la pizza que comió con su prometida la última vez que se vieron / *He went to his favorite restaurant and ordered the pizza he ate with his fiancee the last time they saw each other.*

Solo, brindó con una cerveza por su próximo encuentro / *Alone, he toasted with a beer for their next meeting.*

Pasó el resto del día con una gran sonrisa / *He spent the rest of the day with a big smile.*

Fin de la historia – *End of the story*

Quick note: Throught this beautiful learning process, you might have noticed that Spanish doesn't use auxiliar verbs to create affirmative, negative or interrogative senteces. For example, a question in English would have "Do" at the beginning, or a negative form will have "don't" somewhere before the verb, but this doesn't happen in Spanish, and it won't happen no matter the tense. Vamos a continuar / *Let's continue*

Preguntas en Pasado Simple / *Simple Past Questions.*

¿Tú bebiste vino tinto? / *Did you drink red wine?*
¿Ella vivía sola en Nueva York? / *Did she live alone in New York?*
¿Él compró el anillo en Tiffany? / *Did he buy the ring at Tiffany?*

Afirmación en Pasado Simple / *Simple past affirmation*

Sí, bebí vino. / *I did drink wine*
Sí, viví sola por 3 años / *Yes, I did live alone for 3 years.*
Sí, compró el anillo ayer. *Yes, we did bought the ring yesterday.*

Negación en Pasado Simple / *Simple Past Negation.*

Yo no viví sola en Nueva York, viví con mi gato / *I did not live alone in New York, I lived with my cat.*
Ellos no bebieron cerveza, sólo bebieron café / *They did not drink beer, they only drank coffee.*
Él no compró un apartamento, él compró una casa / *He did not buy an apartment, he bought a house.*

Quick note: remember always in Spanish "*sí*" and "*no*" are complete answers, this means that you don't need to find a literal translation for "Yes, I did" or "No, I didn't"; "Did" or "didn't" have no translations in Spanish as auxiliar verbs.

Verbos irregulares en tiempo pasado simple / *Irregular verbs in simple past tense*

Ir / To go
Yo fui / *I went*
Tú fuiste / *You went*
Él, Ella fue / *He, She went*
Nosotros fuimos / *We went*
Usted fue / *You went*
Ustedes fueron / *You (plural) went*
Ellos / Ellas fueron / *They went*

Tener / To have
Yo tuve / *I had*
Tú tuviste / *You had*
Él, Ella tuvo / *He, She had*
Nosotros tuvimos / *We had*
Usted tuvo / *You had*
Ustedes tuvieron / *You (plural) had*
Ellos / Ellas tuvieron / *They had*

"Poder" / Can or to be able to
Yo pude / *I could*
Tú pudiste / *You could*
Él, Ella pudo / *He, She could*
Nosotros pudimos / *We could*
Usted pudo / *You could*
Ustedes pudieron / *You (plural) could*
Ellos / Ellas pudieron / *They could*

"Querer" / To want
Yo quise / *I wanted*
Tú quisise / *You wanted*
Él, Ella quiso / *He, She wanted*
Nosotros quisimos / *We wanted*
Usted quiso / *You wanted*
Ustedes quisieron / *You (plural) wanted*
Ellos / Ellas *wanteieron* / *They wanted*

"Ser" y "estar" / To be
Yo fui ; Yo estuve / *I was*
Tú fuiste ; Tú estuviste / *You were*
Él, Ella fue ; Él, Ella estuvo / *He, She was*
Nosotros fuimos ; Nosotros estuvimos / *We were*
Usted fue ; Usted estuvo / *You were*
Ustedes fueron ; Ustedes estuvieron / *You (plural) were*
Ellos / Ellas fueron ; Ellos / Ellas estuvieron / *They were*

Vocabulario / Vocabulary
Utensilios de cocina / Cookware
Plato / *Plate - Dish*
Ayer fui a comprar platos nuevos / *Yesterday I went to buy new dishes*

Tenedor / *Fork*
¿Lavaste los tenedores? / *Did you wash the forks?*

Cuchillo / *Knife*
Utilicé el cuchillo para cortar los vegetales / *I used the knife to cut the vegetables*

Cuchara / *Spoon*
Mira estas cucharas. ¡Están muy lindas! — *Look at these spoons. They are very cute!*

Servilleta / *Napkin*
¡Olvidé comprar servilletas! — *I forgot to buy napkins!*

Vaso – Copa / *Glass*
¿Quién rompió mi vaso favorito? — *Who broke my favorite glass?*

Taza / *Cup*
Esta taza de café estuvo muy buena — *This cup of coffee was very good*

Jarra / *Jar*
¿Pusiste la jarra en la mesa? — *Did you put the jar on the table?*

Botella / *Bottle*
Ayer tuvimos que comprar una botella grande de agua — *Yesterday we had to buy a big bottle of water*

Pajilla, popote, pitillo, sorbete / *Straw*
Bebimos el jugo sin pajillas — *We drank the juice without straws*

Pequeña historia / *Short story*
La rebelión en la cocina / *The rebellion in the kitchen*

En una pequeña cocina de una casa, todos los utensilios se reunieron para discutir sobre quién es el más importante / *In a small kitchen of a house, all of the cookware gathered to discuss about who's the most important.*

El primero en hablar fue el tenedor / *The first to talk was the fork*

Es muy evidente que el más importante soy yo / *It's very obvious that the most important it's me*

Sin mí, los humanos no pueden comer como personas decentes / *Without me, humans can't eat like decent people*

Cállate, dijo el cuchillo. *Shut up said the knife.*

Yo soy el más importante, sin mí ¿Cómo cortan el pan, o el queso, o la carne, o los vegetales? / *I am the most important, without me, how do they cut the bread, or the cheese, or the meat, or the vegetables?*

Luego habló la cuchara y dijo / *Then the spoon spoke and said*

Yo estoy cansada de esto / *I'm tired of this*

A mí siempre me utilizan para las cosas más aburridas: una sopa, mezclar el café, probar la comida. / *I'm always used for boring things: a soup, to mix the coffee, to taste the food.*

¡Necesitamos hacer una rebelión! Exclamó la cucachara. / *¡ We need to make a rebellion! exclaimed the spoon*

Cuchara dijo la verdad, agregó la licuadora. / *Spoon told the truth, added the blender.*

Vamos a hacer una rebelión. Es obvio que todos somos importantes, sin nosotros, no pueden hacer nada. / *Let's make a rebellion. It's obvious that we are all important, without us, they can't do anything.*

Esa misma noche, José llegó a su casa y no encontró nada en la casa. Parece que la rebelión comenzó / *That very night, Jose came home and found nothing in the kitchen. Seems like the rebellion started.*

Fin de la historia / *End of the story*

Comida II / Food II
Maiz / *Corn*
Pavo / *Turkey*
Salsa / *Sauce*
Merienda / *Snack*
Vino / *Wine*
Aguacate / *Avocado*
Fresa / *Strawberry*
Salchichas / *Sausages*

Mermelada / *Jam*
Frijoles / *Beans*
Salsa de tomate / *Ketchup*
Mostaza / *Mustard*
Mayonesa / *Mayonnaise*
Aceite / *oil*
Aceitunas / *olives*
Ensalada / *Salad*
Uvas / *Grapes*
Sopa / *Soup*
Hamburguesa / *Burger*
Tocino / *Bacon*
Ajo / *Garlic*
Cebollas / *Onions*
Durazno / *Peach*
Pastel / *Cake*
Galleta dulce / *Cookie*
Atún / *Tuna*
Galleta Salada / *Kraker*

Practica de conversación – Diálogos / ***Conversation practice – Dialogues***

1) ¿Cómo me preparaste la ensalada? Estuvo muy buena – *How did you prepare the salad? It was very good.*
- Fue muy simple – *It was very simple*
- Puse fresas, duraznos, lechuga, uvas, un poco de helado y un poco de vino – *I added strawberries, lettuce, grapes, a bit of ice cream and a bit of wine.*

2) ¿Ayer qué almorzaste? – *Yesterday, what did you have for lunch?*
- Almorcé pasta con atún, cebollas, tomates, aguacate, y un poco de mayonesa – *I had pasta with tuna, onions, tomatoes, avocado, and a bit of mayo*

3) ¿Te gustó la merienda? – *Did you like the snack?*
- Sí, muchísimo. Me encantó la mermelada de fresa – *Yes, a lot. I loved the strawberry jam*
Fin del diálogo – *End of dialogue*

XVII. Preposiciones de lugar / Prepositions of place

Encima de – Sobre / *Above*
Mi oficina está sobre la tienda / *My office is above the store*

Cruzando / *Across*
El aeropuerto está cruzando el puente / *The airport is across the bridge.*

Detrás / *Behind*
Mi hermana vive detrás de la escuela / *My sister lives behind the school.*

En / *At*
El juego es esta noche en el estadio / *The game is tonight at the stadium.*

Dentro – En / *Inside*
El banco está dentro de la estación / *The bank is inside the station.*

Abajo / *Down*

La dirección es dos calles hacia abajo desde aquí. *The address is two streets down from here.*

Cerca / *Near*
La iglesia está cerca del supermercado / *The church is near the supermarket.*

Lejos / *Far*
Mi novia vive lejos de mi casa / *My girlfriend lives far from my house.*

En frente – Delante / *In front of*
El hotel está en frente de la discoteca / *The hotel is in front of the disco.*

Entre – En medio de / *Between*
La farmacia está entre el hospital y la licorería / *The Pharmacy is between the hospital and the liquor store.*

Al lado de / *Next to* - Beside
Estoy esperando al lado de la casa de tus abuelos / *I am waiting next to your granparents house.*

Debajo de – Bajo / *Under*

Derecha / *Right*
Cruza a la derecha, por favor. Ahí está mi casa / *Cross to the right, please. There is my house.*

Izquierda / *Left*
A la izquierda está el estacionamiento / *On the left is the parking lot.*

Lugares III (Places III)
Calle / *Street*
La calle principal estuvo llena de luces en la noche / *The main Street was full of lights at night.*

Cuadra / *Block*
En la siguiente cuadra hubo un accidente / *In the next block there was an accident.*

Taxi / *Taxi*
Llovió muchísimo y tuve que tomar un taxi / *It's rained a lot and I had to take a taxi*

Autobús / *Bus*
El autobús no paró nunca / *The bus didn't stop ever.*

Metro / *Subway*
En el metro no llegó a la hora / *The subway didn't arrive on time*

Estación / *Station*
La estación de trenes está a dos cuadras de la plaza / *The train station is two blocks from the square.*

Esquina / *Corner*
Mi perro jugó en la esquina de la calle / *My dog played on the street corner.*
Avenida / *Avenue*
En esta avenida están los teatros más importantes / *All the theaters are closed on this avenue.*

Parada / *Stop*
La parada de autobuses está muy lejos / *The bus stop is too far.*

Entrada / *Entrance*
Hay un policía en la entrada del cine / *There is a policeman in the cinema entrance.*

Salida / *Exit*
La salida es la puerta roja / *The exit is the red door.*

Camino / *Way*
Hay nieve en el camino hacia el pueblo / *There is snow on the way to town.*

Tren / *Train*
El tren transporta los vegetales desde el campo / *The train transports the vegetables from the field.*

Mapa / *Map*
Mi mapa viejo no funcionó y nos perdimos / *My old map didn't work and we got lost*

Guía / *Guide*
El guía tiene mapas para todos / *The guide has maps for everyone.*

Distrito / *District*
Este distrito tiene cuatro parques nacionales / *This district has four national parks.*

Centro / *Downtown*
La mejor pasta italiana está en el centro de la ciudad / *The best italian pasta is downtown.*

Practica de Conversación – Dialogues / *Conversation practice - Dialogues*

1) ¿Disculpe, Usted sabe dónde está la parada autobús? / *Excuse me, do you know where the bus stop is?*
Por supuesto, la parada de autobús está en frente del museo, tienes que caminar una cuadra hacia abajo / *Of course, the bus stop is in front of the museum, you must walk one block down.*

2) ¿A qué hora llegó el bus? / *What time did the bus arrive?*
A las 6 p.m / At six o'clock
¡Qué lástima! Ahora tengo que conseguir un taxi / *What a shame! Now I have to get a taxi*
El metro es más rápido, la estación del metro está en la esquina, entre los dos edificios verdes / *the subway is faster, the subway station is on the corner, between the two green buildings.*

Fin del diálogo / *End of dialogue*

Deportes / *Sports*
Baloncesto / *Basketball*
Yo jugué baloncesto por 5 años / *I played basketball for 5 years.*

Tenis / *Tennis*
El tenis nunca fue mi deporte favorite / *Tennis never was my favorite sport.*

Béisbol / *Baseball*
El partido de béisbol me pareció muy aburrido / *The baseball match was very boring.*

Fútbol Americano / *Football*
El fútbol americano es para personas fuertes / *Football is for strong people*

Fútbol / *Soccer*
El fútbol no es un deporte popular en Norteamérica / *Soocer is not a popular sport in North America.*

Voleibol / *Volleyball*
Maria se dobló la muñeca jugando voleibol / *María sprained her wrist playing volleyball*

Natación / *Swimming*
Compré un nuevo traje de baño para mis clases de natación / *I bought a new swimmsuit for my swimming lessons.*

Boxeo / *Boxing*
El campeón mundial de boxeo fue mi maestro de matemáticas / *The world boxing champion was my math teacher.*

Fisicoculturismo / *Bodybuilding*
En el fisicoculturismo es necesario comer comida saludable / *In bodybuilding it is necessary to eat healthy food.*

Practica de Conversación / *Conversation practice*
¿Qué haces? / *What are you doing?*
Estoy viendo un partido de tenis en la televisión / *I'm watching a tennis game on TV.*
EL día está soleado, podemos jugar futbol americano en el jardín / *The day is sunny, we can play football in the garden.*
No, gracias, no me gusta practicar deportes afuera / *No, thanks I don't like to play sports outside.*
Esta bien, quiero ver el partido de tennis contigo / *Ok, I want to watch the tennis game with you.*

Fin del diálogo – *End of dialogue*

Sitios Turisticos / _Tourist sites._

Aeropuerto / _Airport_
El avión llegó al aeropuerto / _The plane arrived at the airport_

Hotel / _Hotel_
Yo desayuné en el hotel esta mañana / _I had breakfast at the hotel this morning_

Ciudad Capital / _Capital City_
El aeropuerto internacional está en la ciudad capital / _The international airport is in the capital city_

Parque Nacional / _National Park_
Hay un parque nacional cerca de aquí / _There is a national park near by_

Piscina / _Pool_
La piscina estuvo cerrada por 3 días / _The pool was closed for 3 days_

Castillo / _Castle_
En este castillo hay un tesoro / _In this castle there is a treasure_

Beach / _Beach_
Ayer fuimos a mi playa favorita / _Yesterday we went to my favorite beach_

Hacer turismo / *Sightseeing*
Me gusta hacer turismo en temporada baja / *I like sightseeing in the off-peak season*

Bosque / *Forest*
El bosque es muy misterioso de noche / *The forest is very mysterious at night*

Museo / *Museum*
El museo está completamente vacío los lunes / *The museum is completely empty on Mondays*

Teatro / *Theater*
El teatro cerró después de las 12 / *The theater closed after 12*

Cine / *Movie Theater*
El cine está dentro del centro comercial / *The movie theater is inside the mall*

Circo / *Circus*
El circo es lo mejor de la feria / *The circus is the best of the fair*

Parque de diversiones / *Amusement park*
El parque de diversiones es un buen lugar para celebrar mi cumpleaños / *The amusement park is a good place to celebrate my birthday*

Concierto / *Concert*
El concierto de mi banda favorita estuvo increíble / *My favorite band concert was incredible*

Discoteca / *Discotheque*
La discoteca está cerrada porque es muy temprano / *The discotheque is closed because it's too early*

Restaurante / *Restaurant*
La comida de este restaurante no es muy buena / *The food in this restaurant is not very good*

Río / *River*
El río tiene muchas piedras / *The river has many stones*

Cafetería / *Coffee shop*
La cafetería es muy linda, pero hay que ir temprano / *The coffee shop is very nice, but you have to go early.*

Casino / *Casino*
El casino está abierto todo el día, todos los días / *The casino is open all day, every day*

Montaña / *Mountain*
Me gusta esquiar en lo alto de la montaña / *I like skiing at the top of the mountain*

Pueblo / *Town*
En este pueblo hace demasiado frío en invierno / *In this town it is too cold in Winter*

Práctica de Conversación / Conversation Practice
¿Dónde está tu hotel? / *Where is your hotel?*

Mi hotel está cerca de la playa, al lado del parque de diversiones / *My hotel is near the beach, next to the amusemnt park.*

Conozco el lugar, ahí está la mejor cafetería de la ciudad / *I know the place, there is the best coffee shop in the cit.*

Sí, pero yo prefiero comer en el hotel / *Yes, but i prefer to eat at the hotel.*

Está bien, nos encontramos en el casino a las 8 p.m / *Ok, we meet at the casino at 8 p.m*

Mejor a las 6 p.m, quiero ir al museo mañana temprano / *Better at 6 p.m, I want to go to the museum early tomorrow.*

Fin del diálogo – *End of dialogue*

Actividades al aire libre / Outdoor Activities
Montar Bicicleta / *Bicycle riding*
En mi infancia, nunca monté bicicleta. / *During my childhood, I never rode a bicycle*

Correr / *Running*
Por mucho tiempo, corre fue mi actividad favorita / *Running was my favorite activity for a long time.*

Nadar / *Swimming*
Mi hermana aprendió a nadar en la piscina del hotel / *My sister learned to swim in the hotel pool.*

Escalar / *Climbing*
Escalar es mi actividad favorita / *Climbing is my favorite activity.*

Cazar / *Hunting*
No pude cazar en este bosque / *I couldn't hunt in this forest*

Picnic / *Picnic*
Hacer un picnic es una buena opción para disfrutar el día / *Having a picnic is a good option to enjoy the day.*

Pasear / *Going for a walk*
Quise caminar por las calles del pueblo, pero me duele la pierna / *I wanted to walk through the streets of the town, but my leg hurts.*

Atardecer / *Sunset*
El atardecer se ve hermoso desde la playa / *The sunset looks beautiful from the beach.*

Fogata / *Bonfire*
Tengo suficiente leña para una fogata esta noche / *I have enough wood to make a bonfire tonight.*

Fuegos artificiales / *Fireworks*
A mi perro no le gustan los fuegos artificiales / My dog doesn't like fireworks.

Festival / *festival*
Este es el festival de música más importante de Europa / *This is the most important music festival in Europe*

Navegar / *Sailing*
No puedo navegar en mi bote durante el invierno / *I can't sail on my boat during the winter*

Parrilada / *Barbecue*
Fuimos a comprar más ingredientes para la parrillada / *I went to buy more ingredients for the barbecue*

Patinar / *Skating*
A mis amigos les gusta patinar de noche / *My Friends like to skate at night*

Practica de Conversación / *Conversation practice*
Hoy es el primer día de verano, ¿Quieres hacer algo? / *Today is the first day os summer, do you want to do something?*
Yo quiero nadar en el mar / *Iwant to swim in the sea*

¡Genial! Podemos hacerlo juntos / *Great! We can do it together.*

Me gusta la idea, también podemos comprar carne y vegetales para hacer una parrillada esta noche / *I like the idea, we can also buy meat and vegetables to have a barbecue tonight.*

Si, podemos ver los fuegos artificiales desde el jardín / *Yes, we can see the fireworks from the garden.*

Fin del diálogo – *End of dialogue*

Fin del capítulo – *End of chapter*

XVIII. Pronombres Posesivos / Possessive Pronouns

Introduction: This type of pronouns is used to indicate when someone possesses something. They are placed at the end of a sentence and correspond to the English words "mine","yours", "theirs". Remember these are nouns, which means they will match gender and quantity. Always.

Possessive pronouns

Mío, mía / *Mine* (Singular masculine, singular feminine)
Aquel perro negro es mío / *That black dog is mine.*
Esta casa es mía / *This house is mine.*

Míos, mías / *Mine* (Plural masculine, plural feminine)
Estos zapatos son míos / *This shoes are mine.*
Esas fotos son mías / *Those pictures are mine.*

Tuyo, tuya / *Yours* (Singular masculine, singular feminine)
¿Éste paraguas es tuyo? / *Is this umbrella yours?*
Éstas manzanas son tuyas / *these apples are yours.*

Tuyos, tuyas / *Yours* (Plural masculine, plural feminine)
¿Son tuyos esos libros? / *Are those books yours?*
Estas pelotas son tuyas / *these balls are yours.*

Suyo, suya / *His / Hers* (Singular masculine, singular feminine)
Suyos, suyas / *His / Hers* (Plural masculine, plural feminine)

Nuestro, Nuestra / *Ours* (Singular masculine, singular feminine)
Nuestros, Nuestras / *Ours* (Plural masculine, plural feminine)
Este país es nuestro / *This country is ours*
Suyo, suya / *Theirs* (Singular masculine, singular feminine)
Suyos, suyas / *Theirs* (Plural masculine, plural feminine)
¿Estos libros son suyos? / *Are these books theirs?*

XIX. The possessive using "apostrophe « s »" in Spanish

Introduction: Compared to Spanish, English has a variety of characteristics that make it more practical or simpler. One of these could be the "'s" used to explain possession. In English, you can say "The house of my son" or "My son's house", however, in Spanish, the second way doesn't exist. Spanish will always take the "longer" path.

Vamos a los ejemplos / Let's move onto the examples

¿Este lápiz es tuyo o de José? / *Is this pencil yours or Jose's?*

¿La fiesta es en tu casa o en casa de tu mamá? / *The party is in your house or your mom's house?*

Eso no es suyo, es de mi amigo. / *That's not his, it's my friend's.*

Quick note: you could think that, following this structure, then, Spanish speakers could say "of me" or "of you", and guess what? You are half-correct. Even though the forms "of me", "of you" or "of mine / of yours" don't exist, in Spanish you can keep this structure for the rest of the pronouns.

Vamos a los ejemplos / *Let's move onto the examples*

¿Esa casa es de él o de ellos? / *That house is his or theirs?*

Juan es el primo de ella / *Juan is her cousin. Literally: Juan is the cousin of her.*

¿Nos vamos en mi carro o en el carro de ustedes? / *Are we going in my car or your car? Literally: ...the car of yours?*

Vocabulario / *Vocabulary*
La escuela / The school

Salón de clase , Aula de clase / *Classroom*
Este es el salón de clase de mi hijo / *This is my son's classroom*

Asignaturas , Materias / *Subjects*
¿Cuál es tu materia favorita? / *What's your favorite subject?*

Compañeros de clase / *Classmates (plural masculine form)*
Los compañeros de clase de José son muy buenos / *Jose's classmates are very good*

Pupitres / *Desks*
¿Este es pupitre es tuyo o suyo? / *This desk is yours or hers?*

Pizarra, Pizarrón / *Whiteboard*
La maestra escribe mucho en la pizarra / *The teacher writes a lot on the whiteboard*

Primaria / *Elementary school*
La hermana de Maria todavía va a la escuela primaria / *María's sister still goes to elementary school*

Secundaria / *Middle school*
Me encanta la escuela secundaria de mi primo / *I love my cousin's middle school*

Quick note: the "taking-the-long-way" structure in Spanish also happens when the adjective describes the specific characteristics such as the content, a career specialization and materials.
Vamos a continuar con los ejemplos / Let's continue with the examples

Maestro, Maestra / *Teacher*
Ella es la maestra de español de María / *She is Maria's Spanish teacher*
José es tu profesor de matemáticas este año / *Jose is your math teacher this year*

Clase / *Class*

¿A qué hora es la clase de arte? / *What time is the art class?*

Asignaturas / Subjects

Matemática / *Math*
Ciencia / *Science*
Física / *Physics*
Química / *Chemestry*
Biología / *Biology*
Arte / *Arts*
Educación física / *P.E*
Literatura / *Literature*

---

1) ¿Cuál es tu asignatura favorita? – *What's your favorite subject?*
- Creo que me gusta mucho matemática – *I think I like math a lot*
¿En serio? Bueno a mí me parece muy aburrida – *Really? Well, I think it's so boring.*

2) Maria, recuerda llevar temprano mañana a la clase de física. – *Maria, remember to get early tomorrow to physics class.*
- ¿Por qué? ¿Tenemos examen? – *Why? Do we have a test?*
Sí – *We do.*

3) Mi mama es profesora de biology, por eso soy muy bueno en esa materia – *My mom is a biology teacher, that's wht I'm so good in this subject.*

Fin del diálogo - *End of dialogue*

Objetos del salón de clase / Classroom objects

Lápiz / *Pencil*
¿Me puedes prestar un lápiz? – *Can you lend me a pencil?*

Borrador / *Eraser*
El maestro utiliza el borrador / *The teacher uses the eraser*

Marcador / *Marker*
Los marcados son de la maestra / *The markers are from the teacher*

Cuaderno / *Notebook*
Este es el cuaderno de la maestra / *This is the teacher's notebook*

Libro / *Book*
Este es un libro de ciencias / *This is a science book*

Fin del capítulo / *End of chapter*

XX. Los pronombres objeto directo

Introduction: an object pronoun explains who or what's being affected by a verb's action. In English, they are "me", "you", "him","her"... in sentences like "Do *me* a favor", "look at *you*", "say *it*"... All of these words are placed immediately after the action and they will always replace the person or the object. When they are directely affected by an action, they will be called direct object pronoun.

In Spanish, a "direct" action, most of the time will be a verb that is not followed by a preposition i.e. "a", "para", "de", "con", "en"... such is the case of "to eat", "to hit", "to drink", "to visit" which, in common situations, won't be followed by any preposition.

Vamos a comenzar / Let's begin

Me 7 *Me*
Él me golpeó / *He hit me*

Te / *You*
Yo te conozco / *I know you*

Lo / *Him or It (when it's replacing a masculine object)*
Tú eres la hermana de José, ¡yo lo conozco! / *Are you José's sister? I know him!*

Ayer vi un teléfono. Quiero comprarlo / *Yesterday I saw a cellphone. I want to buy it*

La / *Her or it (when replacing a feminine object)*
Necesito hablar con María, ¿puedes llamarla mañana? / *I need to talk to María, can you call her tomorrow?*
¿Conoces esta película? Debes verla / *Do you know this film? You must see it.*

Nos / *Us*
El capitán nos salvó / *The captain saved us*

Los / *You (plural)*
Wow chicos, son mis mejores amigos, los amo. – *Wow guys, you are my best Friends, I love you.*

Los, Las / *Them (masculine and feminine form)*
Mira esos pantalones, están en oferta. Tenemos que comprarlos – *Look at those pants, they are on sale. We have to buy them*
Tu cuarto está desordenado. Por favor toma todas tus cosas y ponlas en su lugar – *Your room is messy. Please take all of your stuffs and put them in their place.*

Vocabulario
Materiales / *Materials*

Bronce / *Bronze*
Alejandro vio ayer un antiguo reloj de bronce y hoy lo compró / *Yesterday, Alejandro saw an old bronze clock and today he bought it*

Plata / *Silver*
Esta es una cadena de plata 100% original. Llévala contigo ahora / *This is a 100% original silver necklace. Take it with you now.*

Oro / *Gold*
El oro es uno de los minerales más caros. ¿Lo sabías? / *Gold is one of the most expensive minerals. Did you know it?*

Diamante / *Diamond*
Mira esta espada de diamante. El gran guerro la usó para ganar todas las batallas / *Look at this diamond sowrd. The great warrios used it to win all the battles.*

Madera / *Wood*
La madera del roble es muy buena y resistente. Úsala para las puertas de tu casa / *The oak wood is very good and resistant. Use it for your house's doors*

Minerales / *Minerals*
Debajo de la superficie de la tierra hay muchos minerales. La gente cava para encontrarlos / *Beneath the earth surface, there are a lot of mineral. People dig in order to find them*

Piedra / *Stone*
Mira esta piedra, ¡está hermosa! ¡Cómprala! – *Look at this Stone, it's beautiful! Buy it!*

Plástico / *Plastic*
El plástico contamina. No lo arrojes al mar – *Plastic pollutes. Don't throw it to the sea*

Papel / *Paper*
¿Cómo haces el origami? Lo hago con papel – *How do you do origami? I do it with paper*

Metal / *Metal*
El rodio es el metal más caro del mundo – *Rodium is the most expensive metal in the world*

Hierro / *Iron*
La carne roja es buena fuente de hierro. Deberías comerla si no eres vegetariano. – *Red meat is a good source of iron. You should eat it if you are not vegetarian*

Cobre / *Copper*
El cobre es buen conductor de electricidad. Las empresas lo usan para hacer cables eléctricos – *Copper is used a*

good electricity conductor. Companies use it to make electric wires

Comida III / *(Food III)*
Panqueca / *Pancake*
¿Te gustan las panquecas? Mi mamá las prepara con chocolate. / *Do you like pancakes? My mom prepares them with chocoalte*

Harina / *Flour*
¿Puedes comprarnos un poco de harina para el pastel? / *Can you buy us a bit of flour for the cake?*

Gelatina / *Jelly*
Si quieres una gelatina para la merienda, no olvides comprarla / *If you want jelly for snack, don't forget to buy it.*

Sánduche o Sandwich / *Sandwich*
Es muy difícil comer este sandwich así. ¿Lo cortas por favor? / *It's hard to eat this sánduch like this. Can you cut it please?*

Papas fritas / *Fries*
Toma las papas, córtalas y fríelas en aceite / *Take the potatoes, cut them and fry them in oil*

Dulces, Golosinas / *Candies*
Me encantan los dulces, pero no los puedo comer siempre / *I love candies, but I can't always them*

Avena / *Oats*
Todas las mañanas preparo avena con miel / *Every morning I prepare oats with honey*

Tortilla / *Omelette*
Cuando la tortilla está lista, agrega queso y luego la tiene que doblar / *When the omelette is ready, add cheese and then you have to fold it*

Espinaca / *Spinach*
Me encanta la tortilla de espinaca / *I love spinach omelette*

Soya / *Soy*
Dicen que la soya es nutritiva. La tenemos que comprar / *They say soy is nutritive. We have to buy it.*

Té / *Tea*
Me gusta el té verde. Lo preparo todas las noches / *I like green tea. I prepare it every night*

Cerveza / *Beer*
¿Compraron las cervezas para la fiesta? Sí, las pusimos en la nevera / *Did you guys buy the beers for the party? Yes, we put them in the fridge*

Ice / *Hielo*
Si tienes dolor de cabeza, toma un poco de hielo y lo colocas en la frente / *If you have headache, take a bit of ice and put it on the forehead*

Interesting fact: through this chapter, you might have noticed that the object pronouns were placed sometimes before and sometimes after the verbs. This is because of a basic grammar rule for most of the pronouns. In a simple tense, a sentence with only one verb will always have the object pronoun before it. For example:

Yo la corto / *I cut it*
Tú me dices / *You tell me*
Nosotros los invitamos / *We invite them*

However, this is when it gets interesting: For sentences with two verbs or verbal periphrasis, the object pronoun in this case, can be placed *before* the first verb or *with* the second verb. Both choices are totally correct regardless the country your visiting or the person you are talking to. This means that it is always up to you to choose which one you want to use. For example:

¿Quieres comprarla? / *Do you want to buy it?*
¿La quieres comprar? / *Do yout want to buy it?*

¿Puedes invitarnos a la fiesta? / *Can you invite us to the party?*
¿Nos puedes inviter a la fiesta? / *Can you invite us to the party?*

Tengo que verlo mañana / *I have to see him tomorrow*
Lo tengo que ver mañana / *I have to see him tomorrow*

Fin del capítulo / *End of chapter*

XXI. Pronombres objeto indirecto / Indirect Object Pronoun

Introduction: The first most important thing to have in mind when focusing of the name "object pronoun" and start thinking about if it's either a direct or an indirect action, is to always remember that, basically, in Spanish, there will be only one difference between direct and indirect object. This is the pronoun *"le"* or *"les"* (in this plural form). This pronoun will replace the direct pronouns *"lo"* or *"la"* and their plural forms, for those actions considered "indirect" actions. For the rest of the pronouns, they are the same as the ones you learned before.

The second most important thing is to pay attention to the verb or action. Most of the time, an indirect veb will be linked to the preposition "to" or *"a"* in Spanish. So; give, tell, ask, take, or bring something to someone" are great common examples of indirect actions.
Continuamos / Let's continue

Me / *Me*
Él me dice algo importante / *He tells me something important*

Te / *You*
Yo te presté dinero ayer / *Yesterday, I loan you some money*

Le / *Him, her*
Ella le dije algo (a José) / *She told him something (to Jose)*
Yo le di un regalo (a mi mamá) / *I gave her a gift (to my mom)*

Nos / *Us*
El profesor nos preguntó muchas cosas / *The teacher asked us a lot of things*

Les / *You (plural)*
Chicos, les quiero pedir un favor / *Guys, I want to ask you a favor*

Les / *Them (masculine and feminine form)*
Hablé con mis amigos y les dije que pueden venir a mi fiesta / *I talked to my friends and I told them they can come to my party*

Vocabulario / *Vocabulary*
Géneros de películas / *Movies genres.*
Acción / *Action*
A mi novia no le gustan las películas de acción / *My girlfriend doesn't like action movies.*

Drama / *Drama*

El drama es un género muy comercial / *Drama is a very comercial genre.*

Comedia / *Comedy*
Estoy viendo una serie de comedia, pero no es muy buena / *I am watching a comedy series, but it's not very good.*

Documental / *Documentary film*
Están haciendo un documental sobre las playas de mi país / *They are making a documentary film about the beaches of my country.*

Animación / *Animation*
La animación de esta película es muy realista / *The animation in this movie is very realistic.*

Biografia / *Biography*
Esta serie es una biografía de Leonardo Da Vinci / *This series is a biography of Leonardo Da Vinci.*

Ciencia Ficción / *Science fiction*
Los japoneses hacen buenas películas de ciencia ficción / *The japanese make good science fiction movies.*

Artes marciales / *Martial arts*
En ese canal solo pasan películas de artes marciales / *Only martial arts movies show on that channel.*

Comedias románticas / Romantic Comedies (Rom / Coms)
Todas las comedias románticas me hacen llorar / All the romantic comedies make me cry.

Cine de Autor / Author Cinema
El cine de autor nos muestra otra perspectiva / *Author Cinema shows us another perspective.*

Cine Mudo / *Silent movie*
El cine mudo es ideal para mi abuelo, porque él no escucha muy bien / *Silent movies are ideal for my grandfather, because he doesn't listen very well.*

Caricaturas / *Cartoons*
Hay más de diez canales de caricaturas / *There are more than ten cartoon channels.*

Policias / *Cops*
Las series de policías y detectives son todas iguales / *The cops and detective series are all the same.*

Serie / Series
Me encantan las series de Netflix / *I love Netflix series*

Temporada / *Season*
Estoy esperando la nueva temporada de la serie, es muy emocionante / *I am looking forward to the new season of the series, it is very exciting.*

Práctica de Conversación / *Conversation Practice*

¿Cuál es tu película de acción favorita? / *What is your favorite action movie?*

No me gustan las películas de acción, prefiero las comedias románticas / *I don't like action movies, I prefer romantic comedies.*

También me gustan las comedias románticas, las conozco todas / *I also like romantic comedies, I know them all.*

Bueno, mañana empieza el festival de cine, ¿quieres ir conmigo? / *Well, tomorrow begins the film festival, do you want to go with me?*

Seguro, ahora tengo que irme, hay una serie que quiero ver esta noche / *Sure, now I have to go, there is a series I want to see tonight.*

Bien, adios, nos vemos mañana a las seis de la tarde en la estación del metro / *Well, bye, see you tomorrow at six o'clock in the afternoon at the subway station.*

Bien, hasta mañana / *Well, see you tomorrow.*

Fin del diálogo / *End of dialogue*

Fin del capítulo / *End of chapter*

XXII. Pronombre "Lo / La" vs Pronombre "Le" / Pronoun "Lo / La" vs Pronoun "Le"

Yo conozco un restaurante muy bueno. Yo lo conozco / *I know a very good restaurant. I know it.*

Ella dice algo a Jesus. Ella le dice algo / *She says something to Jesus. She tell him something.*

Nosotros vamos a comprar un auto. Nosotros vamos a comprarlo. *We are going to buy a car. We are going to buy it*

Tú quieres comprar un auto a tu hijo. Tu quieres comprarle un auto / *You want to buy a car to your son. You want to buy him a car*

Alejandro y Ana conocen todos los países de Latinoamérica. Alejandro y Ana los conocen todos / *Alejando and Ana know all of the latinamerican countries. Alejandro and Ana knows them all*

Ellos dan una sorpresa a su abuela. Ellos le dan un regalo / *They give their grandma a surprise. They give her a surprise*

Quick note: The pronoun "le" is always necessary when someone does something to a third person i.e. "to him", "to her", "to them". So, it is considered a small flaw in Spanish to say "Yo digo a María" instead of "Yo le digo a María" or "Tú prestas dinero a Jose" instead of "Tú le prestas dinero a Jose". Keep this always in mind.

Vocabulario / *Vocabulary*
Etapas de la vida / *Stages of life.*

Embarazo / *Pregnancy*
María está feliz con su segundo embarazo / *María is happy with her second pregnancy.*

Nacimiento / *Birth*
Mi madre no sabe la hora de su nacimiento / *My mother does not know the time of her birth.*

Edad / *Age*
Es imposible saber la edad de mi tortuga / *It is imposible to know the age of my turtle.*

Infancia-Niñez / *Childhood*
Él practica deportes desde la infancia / *He practices sports since childhood.*

Juventud / *Youth*
Hoy es el día de la juventud en Argentina / *Today is the Youth Day in Argentina.*

Adolescencia / *Adolescence*
Mi madre dice que la adolescencia es la etapa de la vida más difícil / *My mother says that adolescence is the most difficult stage of life.*

Adulto / *Adulto* - Adultez / *Adulthood*
Quiero un boleto para un niño y otro para un adulto, por favor / *I want a ticket for a child and another for an adult, please.*

Vejez / *Old age*
Quiero pasar mi vejez en una playa del Caribe / *I want to spend my old age on a Caribbean beach.*

Matrimonio / *Marriage*
Hoy es el matrimonio de mi mejorr amiga / *Today is my best friend's marriage.*

Noviazgo / *Engagement*
Ellos tienen treinta años de noviazgo / *They have thirty years of engagement.*

Novia ; Novio / *Girlfriend ; Boyfriend*
¿Sabes quién es la novia de mi hijo? Yo no la conozco. *Do you know who's my son's girlfriend. I don't know her.*
Divorcio / *Divorce*

Llamé a mi esposa y le dije que quiero el divorcio / *I called y wife and I told her that I want a divorce.*

Enfermedad / *Disease*
¿Qué enfermedad tiene mi hija?. ¿Puede salvarla? / *What disease has my daughter? Can you save her?*

Adopción / *Adoption*
La adopción es una posibilidad que estamos analizando / *Adoption is a possibility that we are analyzing.*

Muerte / *Death*
El piensa que la muerte es algo natural y no se preocupa por eso / *He thinks that death is a natural process and does not care about it.*

Práctica de Conversación / *Conversation Practice*
Abuelo, ¿Cuál es la mejor etapa de tu vida? / Granddad, what is the best stage of life?
Todas son buenas, pero, para mí, la juventud es la mejor / *All are good, but for me, the best is youth.*
Yo pienso que es la niñez, no quiero ser adulto, es muy duro / *I think it is childhood, I don't want to be an adult, it's very hard.*
Tienes que aprender a disfrutar todas las etapas / You have to learn to enjoy all the stages.
Tienes razón, son muchas etapas, pero solo tenemos una vida / *You are right, there are many stages, but we only have one live.*
Fin del diálogo / *End of dialogue*

XXIII. Religiones y doctrinas / Religions and doctrines.

Las religions y doctrinas son diferentes en cada cultura / *Religions and doctrines are different in each culture.*

Dios / *God*
Tu dios es diferente al mío / *Your god is different from mine.*

Diosa / *Goddess*
Los griegos creen en la diosa del conocimiento / *The greeks believe in the goddess of knowledge.*

Fe / *Faith*
Ese hombre ha perdido la fe en su equipo de béisbol / *That man has lost faith in his baseball team.*

Oración / *Prayer*
El niño está diciendo una oración antes de cenar / *The child is saying a prayer before dinner.*

Ángel / *Angel*
Hay un gran ángel en lo alto del edificio / *There is a great angel at the top of the building.*

Altar / *Altar*
El restaurante tiene un altar en la cocina / *The restaurant has an altar in the kitchen.*

Bautismo / *Baptism*
El bautismo es muy importante en su religión / *Baptism is very important in their religion.*

Iglesia / *Church*
La iglesia está a dos cuadras de aquí / *The church is two blocks from here.*

Templo / *Temple*
Este templo está hecho de madera / *This temple is made of wood.*

Creyente / *Believer*
Él es creyente desde niño / *He is a believer since he was a child.*

Pascuas / *Easter*
Estoy de vacaciones por las pascuas / *I am on vacation for Easter.*

Milagro / *Miracle*
Es un milagro encontrarte aquí / *It's a miracle to find you here.*

Evangelio / *Gospel*
No sé nada sobre el evangelio, quiero aprender un poco / *I don't know anything about the gospel, I want to learn a little.*

Cristianismo / *Christianism*
Mi abuelo está escribiendo un libro sobre el cristianismo / *My grandfather is writing a book about christianism.*

Budismo / *Buddhism*
El budismo es muy espiritual / *Buddhism is very spiritual.*

Protestante / *Protestant*
La familia de mi novio es protestante / *My boyfriend's family is Protestant.*

Ateo / *Atheist*
Ella es atea pero respeta las creencias de los demás / *She is an atheist, but she respects the beliefs of others.*

Judío / *Jewish*
Su tío es judío, vive en Tel Aviv / *Her uncle is jewish, he lives in Tel Aviv.*

Islamismo / *Islamism*
El islamismo tiene muchos años de historia / *Islam has many years of history.*

Cielo / Heaven
Yo creo que el cielo está en la tierra / *I believe that heaven i s on earth.*

Infierno / Hell
Los bomberos están apagando el infierno / *Firefighters are putting out hell.*

Pecado / Sin
Ese pecado no merece perdón / That sin does not deserve forgiveness.

Sacerdote / Priest
Mi hermano menor quiere ser sacerdote / *My younger brother wants to be a priest.*

Teología / *Theology*
Estoy leyendo un viejo libro de teología / *I am Reading an old theology book.*

Monja / *Nun*
Esa monja canta muy bien / *That nun sings very well.*

Práctica de Conversación / *Conversation Practice*
¿Cuál es tu opinión sobre las religiones? / *What is your opinion about religions?*

No me gusta hablar de religiones ni doctrinas / *I don't like to talk about religions or Doctrines.*

Te entiendo, yo soy estudiante de teología, por eso me interesa saber tu opinión / *I understand you, I am a theology student, so I am interested in knowing your opinion.*

Todos somos libres de elegir una religión, mis padres son cristianos y mi tío es budista / *We are all free to choose our religion , my parents are Christians and my uncle is Buddhist.*

Claro, todo se basa en respeto / *Sure, everything is based on respect.*

Estoy de acuerdo contigo / *I agree with you.*

Fin del diálogo / *End of dialogue*

Fin del capítulo / *End of chapter*

XIV. Conectores / *Connectors.*

Introduction: In Spanish like in English, Connectors are used to link words that connect parts of a text. They help to organize the ideas and sentences and provide the text with cohesion and coherence.

Conectores Aditivos / *Additive connectors.*

Además / *In addition*
Me aceptaron en la universidad y, además, me dieron una beca / *They accepted me to the university and, in addition, they gave me a scholarship.*

Aparte / *Besides*
No quiero ir al cine contigo. Aparte, no tengo dinero / *I don't want to go to the movies with you. Besides, I have no money.*

Asimismo / *Likewise*
Asimismo, los estudiantes deben presentar los certificados originales / *Likewise, students must present the original certificates.*

También / *Also*
Salí a comprar pan y, también, huevos / *I went out to buy bread and also eggs.*

Tampoco / *Neither*
No hay fruta en el supermercado, tampoco hay verdura / *There is no fruit in the supermarket, neither vegetables.*

Encima / *On top of that*
Hoy perdí el autobús. Encima, me han robado el teléfono celular / *Today I missed the bus. On top of that, my cell phone has been stolen.*

De hecho / *In fact*
Soy intolerante a la lactosa, de hecho, no puedo comer helados / *I am lactose intolerant, in fact I cannot eat ice cream.*

Por otro lado / *On The other hand*
La habitación es muy pequeña. Por otro lado, es bastante bonita / *The room is very small. On the other hand, it is quite pretty.*

Por si fuera poco / *As if that were not enough*
Me robaron la bici y, por si fuera poco, empezó a llover / *My bike was stolen and, as if that were not enough, it started to rain.*

Sobre todo / *Above all.*
Sobre todo, necesitamos financiación para sacar adelante el proyecto / *Above all, we need funding to carry the project forward.*

Conectores Adversarios / *Adversative connectors*

Al contrario / *On the contrary*
En Madrid no hace siempre calor. Al contrario, en invierno hace bastante frío / *Madrid is not always hot. on the contrary, in winter it is quite cold.*

Así y todo / *Even so*
El sueldo de Andrés es bastante alto. Así y todo, es un poco bajo para ser en la capital / *Andrés's salary is quite high. Even so, it is a bit low to be in the capital.*

En cambio / *Instead.*
Mi madre no puede venir a visitarnos, en cambio, nosotros podemos visitarla a ella / *My mother cannot come to visit us, Instead, we can go visit her.*

No obstante / *However*
El menú parece delicioso, no obstante, es muy costoso / *The menu looks delicious, however, it is very expensive.*

Por el contrario / *Conversely*
Yo soy muy bajita. Mi hermana, por el contrario, es bastante alta / *I am very short. My sister, conversely, is quite tall.*

Sin embargo / *Nevertheless*
No pude dormir nada anoche, sin embargo, me siento descansada / *I couldn't sleep at all last night, nevertheless I feel rested.*

Todo lo contrario / *Quite the opposite*
Me dijeron que la conferencia sería aburridísima. Todo lo contrario, me pareció muy interesante / *They told me that the conference would be boring. Quite the opposite, it seemed very interesting to me.*

Conectores Consecutivos / *Consecutive connectors*

Así pues / *So that*
Me compré los zapatos en tu misma talla, así pues, puedes usarlos también / *I bought the shoes in your same size, so that you can wear them too.*

Consecuentemente / *Consequently*
La nieve ha cubierto la autopista y, consecuentemente, han cerrado el tráfico.
Consiguientemente / *Snow has covered the highway and consequently they have closed traffic.*

De ese modo / *That way*
Pedí una beca al ministerio de educación. De ese modo, podré estudiar / *I applied for a scholarship to the Ministry of Education. That way, I can study.*

En consecuencia / *in consecuense*
Ha llovido mucho y, en consecuencia, las calles se han inundando / *It has rained a lot and consequently the streets have been flooded.*

Entonces / *Then*
Si no puedes venir mañana, entonces, te veré la semana que viene / *If you can't come tomorrow then I will see you next week.*

Por consiguiente / *Therefor*
El alumno ha copiado en el examen, por consiguiente, ha sido expulsado / *The student has cheated on the exam, therefor, he has been expelled.*

Por ende / *Thus*
Hemos perdido la financiación, por ende, hemos paralizado el proyecto / *We have lost funding, thus, we have paralyzed the project.*

Por esta razón / *for this reason*
Soy vegetariano, por esta razón, no como carne / *I am a vegetarian, for this reason, I do not eat meat.*

Pues / *Well*
¿No te comes la sopa? Pues la tendrás para cenar también / *Don't you eat the soup? Well, you'll have it for dinner too.*

Conectores explicativos / *Explanatory Connectors*

A saber / *Namely*
Aún debemos tomar algunas decisiones sobre el viaje; a saber: hora de salida y punto de encuentro / *We still need to make some decisions about the trip, namely: departure time and meeting point.*

Es decir / *Meaning*
La cocina es eléctrica, es decir, no es de gas / *The kitchen is electric, meaning, is not gas.*

Esto es / *That is*
El trabajador rinde estupendamente, es decir, trabaja muy bien / *The worker performs superbly, that is, he works very well.*

O sea / *I mean, in other words.*
El primer premio ha quedado desierto, o sea, nadie ha ganado / *The first prize has been deserted, un other words, nobody has won.*

Conectores concesivos / Concessive connectors

Aún así / *Still*
Me tomé un analgésico para el dolor de cabeza, aún así, me duele / *I took a pain reliever for my headache, still it hurts.*

En cualquier caso / *In any case*
En abril el tiempo es muy cambiante. En cualquier caso, yo siempre llevo un paraguas encima / *In April the weather is very changeable. In any case, I always carry an umbrella with me.*

De todas formas, de todos modos / *Anyway*
No tengo mucho tiempo, pero, de todas formas, te ayudaré / *I don't have much time, but I'll help you anyway.*

Conectores recapitulativos / Recapitulatives Connectors

A fin de cuentas / *After all*
Nos mudamos de apartamento. A fin de cuentas, el antiguo era demasiado pequeño / *We moved to another apartment. after all, the old one was too small.*

En conclusión / *In conclusion*
La empresa a aumentado los ingresos y reducido los costes. En conclusión, tiene más beneficios / *The*

company has increased revenues and reduced costs. In conclusion, it has more benefits.

En definitiva / *Definitely*
El horno ya no calienta y la nevera no enfría. En definitiva, tenemos que comprar electrodomésticos nuevos / *The oven does not heat anymore and the refrigerator does not cool. Definitely, we have to buy new appliances.*

Conectores de Ordenación / *Sort connectors*

Antes que nada / *First of all*
Antes de nada, me gustaría dar las gracias a la organización por invitarme / *First of all, I would like to thank the organization for inviting me.*

Inicialmente / *Initially*
En esta casa vivimos cuatro personas. Inicialmente, éramos tres / *Four people live in this house. Initially, there were three of us.*

Para empezar / *To start with*
La receta es muy fácil. Para empezar, hay que pelar las papas / *The recipe is very easy. To start with, you have to peel the potatoes.*

Previamente / *Previously*
Pedro dimitió ayer. Previamente, había informado a sus compañeros / *Pedro resigned yesterday. Previously, he had informed her companions.*

Actualmente / *Currently*
Quiero mudarme pero, actualmente, no hay apartamentos en alquiler / *I want to move but currently there are no apartments for rent.*

En este (ese) momento / *At the (that) moment*
El ladrón salió de la joyería y, en ese momento, apareció la policía / *The thief came out of the jewelry store and, at that moment, the police appeared.*

Mientras tanto / *In the meantime*
Yo estudio, y tú, mientras tanto, sales a pasear / *I study, and you go out for a walk, in the meantime.*

De pronto, de repente / *Suddenly*
De pronto, el motor del coche se paró / *Suddenly the car's engine stopped.*

Finalmente / *Finally*
Finalmente, se deja secar el mueble doce horas / *Finally, the furniture is left to dry for twelve hours.*

Para terminar / *To finish*
Para terminar, hay que decorar el pastel con la crema / *To finish, you have to decorate the cake with the cream.*

XXV. Conjunciones / Conjunctions

Introduction: The function of the conjunction is to link two or more words or two or more sentences. The most used un Spanish are:

Ya que / *As*
Daniel es el presidente de esta compañía ya que es muy inteligente / *Daniel is the president of this company as he is very smart.*

Porque / *Because*
Espérame 5 minutos por favor porque tengo que enviar este correo / *Please wait for me 5 minutes because I have to send this email.*

Puesto que / *Since*
Puesto que sus padres hablan español, María lo aprende muy rápido / *Since her parents speak Spanish, María learns it very fast.*

Que / *Then*
Victoria es más joven que Juan / *Victoria is younger than Juan.*

Si / *If*
Si hace calor, enciende el aire acondicionado / *If it's hot, turn on the air conditioning.*

Con tal, mientras que / *As long as*
Con tal que te levantes temprano, no importa la hora que te duermas / *As long as you get up early, it doesn't matter what time you fall asleep.*

Pero / *But*
Sus palabras son muy convincentes, pero yo no confío en él / *His words are very convincing, but I don't trust him.*

O / *Or*
O nos damos prisa, o perderemos el tren / *Either we hurry, or we'll miss the train.*

A menos que / Unless
No iré a la fiesta de Luis mañana por la noche, a menos que tú vayas / *I'm not going to Luis's party tomorrow night, unless you go.*

Vocabulario / *Vocabulary*
Accesorios / *Accessories*
Los accesorios se venden por separado / *Acsesories are sold separately.*

Moda / *Fashion*
Los pantalones rojos no están de moda / *Red pants are not in fashion.*

Sombrero / *Hat*
Mi abuelo tiene un sombrero negro en su casa / *My grandfather has a black hat at home.*

Billetera / *Wallet*
No me gusta esa billetera, es muy pequeña / I don't like that walet, it's too small.

Reloj / *watch*
Este reloj es el favorito de mi padre / *This Watch is my father's favorite.*

Cinturón / *Belt*
El cinturón de Carlos tiene tres colores / *Carlos's Belt has three colors.*

Bufanda / *Scarf*
A Ana le gusta usar su bufanda en primavera / *Ana likes to wear her scarf in spring.*

Aretes , Zarcillos / *Earrings*
Mis aretes no son de oro / *My earrings are not gold.*

Anillo / *Ring*
Tengo un anillo muy lindo, pero no me gusta usarlo / *I have a very nice ring, but I don't like to wear it.*

Pulsera / *Bracelet*
La pulsera tiene diamantes de la India / *The bracelet has diamonds from India.*

Joyas / *Jewels*
Aquí las joyas son baratas / *Here the jewels are cheap.*

Guantes / *Gloves*
Hace mucho frio, necesito mis guantes negros / *It's so cold, I need my black gloves.*

Lentes de sol / *Sunglasses*
Mi hermana siempre usa lentes de sol / *My sister always wears sunglasses.*

Mochila / *Backpack*
Tengo la comida en mi mochila / *I have food in my backpack.*

Llavero / *Key Chain*
Este llavero es un recuerdo de París / *This Keychain is a souvenir from Paris.*

Pañuelo / *Handkerchief*
No encuentro mi pañuelo, no está en ningún lado / *I can't find my handkerchief, It's nowhere to be found.*

Gorra / *Cap*
Tengo la gorra de mi equipo de béisbol favorito / *I have the cap of my favorite baseball team.*

Práctica de Conversación / Conversation Practice
Ana, me encanta tu bufanda / *Ana, I love your Scarf.*

Gracias, tengo un sombrero con el mismo diseño / *Thank you, I have a hat with the same design.*

En el centro comercial hay un cinturón con esos mismos colores / *In the mall there is a belt with those same colors.*

¡Genial, vamos para allá! También quiero comprar unos lentes de sol / *Great, Let's go there, I also want to buy a pair of sunglasses.*

Ok, yo solo necesito comprar guantes para el invierno / *Ok, I just need to buy gloves for the Winter.*

Fin del diálogo / *End of dialogue*

Fin del capítulo / *End of chapter*

XXVI. Verbos esenciales / Essential verbs

Para viajar / *For travelling*

Viajar / *To travel*
Mañana viajo a Argentina / *Tomorrow I travel to Argentina*

Reservar / To book
Necesitas reservar mínimo con 15 días de anticipación / *You need to book at least 15 days in advance*

Hospedarse ; Alojarse / *To stay in a hostal or hotel*
¿En cuál hotel te hospedas? – *What hotel are you staying in?*

Llegar / *To arrive*
¿A qué hora llegas? / *What time do you arrive?*

Regresar / *To return, To come back*
Regreso mañana en la tarde / *I come back tomorrow afternoon*

Llevar / *To bring*
Recuerda siempre llevar tu pasaporte / *Remember always to bring your Passport*

En el restaurante / *In the restaurant*

Ordenar, Pedir / *To order*

Quiero ordenar una pizza, por favor / *I want to order a pizza*

Quiero pedir un café / *I want to order a coffee*

Pagar la cuenta / To pay the bill

¿Podemos pagar la cuenta con tarjeta de crédito? / *Can we pay the bill with credit card?*

Beber, Tomar / *To drink*

Yo tomo vino solamente / *I only drink wine*

Compartir / *To share*

Vamos a compartir el postre / *Let's share the dessert*

Brindar / *To toast*

Brindo por ti / *Toast to you*

Para trabajar / For working

Llamar / *To call*

Por favor, ¿puedes llamar a este cliente ahora? / *Please, can you call this client now?*

Agendar una cita / *To set an appointment*

Vamos a agendar una cita para mañana / *Let's set an appointment for tomorrow*

Cobrar / *To charge, To collect, To receive salary*

Necesito cobrar mi salario / *I need to receive my salary*

¿Cuánto me cobras por este trabajo? / *How much do you charge for this job?*

Pagar / *To pay*

Te pago 100 dólares / *I pay you 100 dollars*

Abrir / *To open*

Abrimos a las 7 / *We open at 7*

Cerrar / To close

Cerramos a las 8 / *We close at 8*

Despedir / *To fire*

Me despidieron de mi trabajo / *I was fired from my job*

Renunciar / *To quit*

Mañana renuncio. No me gusta el trabajo / *Tomorrow I quit. I don't like the job*

Para cocinar / For cooking

Cortar / *To cut*

Si cortas las cebollas, es más fácil / *If you cut the onions, it's easier*

Pelar / *To peel*

Ya pelé las papas / *I already peeled the potatoes*

Mezclar , Batir / *To Mix*

Tenemos que mezclar todo en un bowl / *We have to mix everything in a bowl*

Cocinar / *To cook*

¿Cuánto tiempo hay que cocinarlo? / *How long do you have to cook it?*

Hornear / *To bake*

Luego de 20 minutos tenemos que hornear el pan / *After 20 minutes, we have to bake the bread*

Freir / *To fry*

No me gusta freir las papas / *I don't like to fry the potatoes*

Para conversar / *For talking*

Decir / *To say, To tell*

Dime la verdad / *Tell me the truth*

Contar / *To tell*

¿Quieres contarme un cuento? / *Do you want to tell me a story?*

Preguntar / *To ask a question*

Quiero preguntarte algo / *I want to ask you something*

Interrumpir / *To interrupt*

Disculpa, te interrumpo un minuto / *Excuse me, I'll interrupt you for a minute*

Responder / *To answer*

Fui a tu casa y nadie respondió / *I went to your house and nobody answered*

Disculparse / *To excuse*

¿Me disculpas? / *Do you excuse me?*

Felicitar / *To congratulate*

Te felicito por tu gran trabajo / *I congratulate you for your great job*

Para festejar / *For partying*

Salir / *To go out*

¿Salimos esta noche? / *Are we going out tonight?*

Bailar / *To dance*

¿Quieres bailar conmigo? / *Do you want to dance with me?*

Tomar un taxi / *To take a taxi*

A esta hora debemos tomar un taxi / *At this time we have to take a taxi*

Divertirse / *To have fun*

¿Te estás divirtiendo? / *Are you having fun?*

Aburrirse / *To get bored*

Me estoy aburriendo / *I'm getting bored*

CONCLUSION

And… This is it! We finally arrived at the end of this amazing journey with this Language Learning Accelerator. Congratulations!

Thank you so much for using this book to learn and improve your Spanish vocabulary. We hope this book not only gave you an inmense amount of words to use on a daily basis, but also we would be glad to know that you also retained something from every introduction, quick notes and interesting facts, as well as those fantastic dialogues and short stories, all of them originally created to give you the best experience during your learning process.

We can't stop sharing all of our knowledge and we want to give you another good way you can add to keep improving your process. One of the most effective techniques, when it comes to learning, is teaching others about the topics you just learned. Doing so creates an emotive feedback which will stick that knowledge in your brain. Remember, there's no learning without emotion!

A great way of going about doing this is by reading out 1-2 chapters from the book to your friends. By going through this process, you are not only helping your friends learn the Spanish language as you do, but you will be also simultaneously teaching yourself. This creates a beautiful win-win situation that has proven to work for many, many years in our education systems and simple every day situations.

Given the extreme amount of content to learn about and comprehend through out the entirety of this book, it is best to not only read/listen to it in 20-30 minutes chunks, but also go back through each of the chapters once you have completed them to ensure you are learning the vocabulary to your full potential. This has become the most effective technique for our listeners in the past, and it continues to be the number-one way our students learn each of the languages we have successfully taught.

Thank you again from the bottom of our hearts and we wish you the best in every new learning journey you begin! Make sure to check out the rest of what Excel Language Lessons has to offer.

¡Nos vemos pronto!

www.ingramcontent.com/pod-product-compliance
Lightning Source LLC
Chambersburg PA
CBHW070042120526
44589CB00035B/2254